Distance Learning Study Guide for

The Way We Live

by

Stephen C. Light, Ph.D.
State University of New York at Plattsburgh

produced by

IN·TELE·COM ®
INTELLIGENT TELECOMMUNICATIONS

The Way We Live is a video-, print-, and web-based course designed and produced by INTELECOM Intelligent Telecommunications

Sociology, 10th Edition, and *Society: The Basics*, 8th Edition, by John Macionis, published by Prentice Hall, are designated for use with this course.

Printed in the United States of America

ISBN 0-13-191403-0

Contents

Preface

The Way We Live is a comprehensive introduction to sociology. It combines the real world immediacy and intimacy of video with the most popular sociology texts available. Noted sociologists provide insights for understanding social groups and institutions, social change, and the sociological forces of daily life. You will visit Delancy Street, an innovative alternative to the correctional system that focuses on rehabilitating instead of simply housing criminal offenders. You will meet the people of the Winnemem Wintu tribe of the Pacific Northwest and learn how government land and water policies have affected them. You will gain perspective about how thoroughly issues of gender saturate daily life in our society through the players on a women's professional football team.

This guide is one part of the total package available to you when you embark on the 22 half-hour videos that make up *The Way We Live*. These video episodes, in conjunction with the guidance of your campus instructor, are closely integrated with John Macionis's texts, *Siociology* and *Society: The Basics*. These texts provide a broad-spectrum introduction to the study of sociology. The newest editions of these books put sociology in a global context, making connections for life in an ever-expanding world.

Each of the half-hour video episodes is accompanied by a complementary lesson in this guide containing the following features to help you master your study of sociology:

— Assignments that link the video lesson with related sections of the text.

— An Overview summarizes each lesson's main topics.

— Learning Objectives identify the major concepts, ideas, and factual data that you should recall and understand after viewing the video and reading the required selections from the text. Many test bank questions are derived from these objectives.

— Key Terms and Concepts help you to focus on the words and ideas important to understanding the language of sociology as you work through each lesson.

— Text Focus Points are intended to guide your reading of the selections for each assignment.

— Video Focus Points help you follow and analyze information in the video and integrate the information with your readings.

— Critical Thinking questions provide opportunities for further examination of the issues raised by the video and readings in the text.

— The Test Your Learning section enables you to check your understanding of the material in the video and text assignments.

Connections

OVERVIEW

The systematic study of human society is termed *sociology*. The *sociological perspective* is a way of looking at life in the social context that involves seeing the general in the particular, meaning that patterns of behavior are identifiable in the actions of individuals. The scientific method is used by sociologists to study human groups and the ways in which the lives of individuals are influenced by the wider society. C. Wright Mills called this approach the *sociological imagination*.

The genesis of sociology was itself driven by sociological change. By the end of the eighteenth century, farmers were abandoning their plows and crowding the cities of England, France, and Germany to find employment in the factories of the dawning industrial revolution. At the same time, a shift from the theological focus of the Middle Ages to the individual rights and liberties climate of America's Declaration of Independence was evolving. Early sociologists like Karl Marx, troubled by this new industrial society, hoped to better understand it and to encourage change in the direction of social justice. It was French social thinker Auguste Comte who first applied the scientific approach to the study of society. In 1838, he coined the term *sociology* to describe this new academic discipline.

Social patterns are more apparent when viewed from a distance, so it is not a coincidence that many of the early contributors of significance to the field of sociology were people on the margins of society due to gender or race—people such as Harriet Martineau, Jane Addams, and W.E.B. Du Bois. During the first decades of the twentieth century sociology became firmly established in American universities.

By applying the sociological perspective in daily life, widely accepted beliefs can be tested against the results of sociological research. The sociological perspective aids in understanding how the decisions made by individuals are influenced by the society in which they live. This is illustrated in the video, "Connections," (Episode 1) which chronicles the difficulties faced by young people from economically disadvantaged backgrounds as they attempt to position themselves for occupational and material success by earning college degrees. The sociological perspective fosters both an objective understanding and an appreciation of cultures and societies— our own and others. By understanding society, we can become more effective participants in it, and we can learn how to change it for the better.

Sociologists create *theories*—statements of how and why specific facts are related—to explain human group life. Theories are tested against real-world data through the research process. The three major theoretical paradigms used in sociology today are symbolic-interactionism, structural-functionalism, and social-conflict theory.

The *structural-functional paradigm* views society as a complex system whose parts work together to promote solidarity and stability. This paradigm focuses on stable patterns of human behavior, or *social structure*. In addition, this perspective examines the consequences of a society's structure on the society as a whole; i.e., its

1

social functions. *Manifest functions* are recognized and intended consequences of a social pattern, while *latent functions* are unrecognized and unintended consequences.

The *social-conflict paradigm* views society as an arena of inequality that generates conflict and change. It assumes that society is structured to benefit powerful persons and groups while keeping the powerless in a deprived position.

Unlike the structural-functional and social-conflict theoretical paradigms, the *symbolic-interaction paradigm* adopts a *micro-level approach*. It focuses on social interaction in everyday situations, and views society as the product of the face-to-face interactions of individuals. One variation of this approach is Erving Goffman's *dramaturgical analysis*, which suggests that much of human behavior resembles a dramatic performance, with actors on a stage playing their assigned roles.

Each of the three theoretical paradigms highlights a different dimension of any social issue or pattern, and provides a way to develop a deeper understanding of the richness of human society.

FOCUS YOUR ATTENTION

Assignments

Read the pages indicated for the text assigned by your instructor.

— *Sociology*, 10th Edition, by Macionis. Chapter 1, "The Sociological Perspective." For additional information on the history of sociology, read Chapter 4, "Sociology."

— *Society: The Basics*, 8th Edition, by Macionis. Chapter 1, "Sociology: Perspective, Theory, and Method," pages 1–17.

Watch Episode 1, "Connections," after scanning the Video Focus Points.

Learning Objectives

After completing your study of this lesson, you should be familiar with the facts and concepts presented and should be able to:

1. Explain how the sociological perspective shows "the general in the particular."

2. Discuss how the sociological imagination enables an understanding of the ways in which the lives of individuals are influenced by the wider society.

3. Describe the benefits of using the sociological perspective, in terms of increasing an understanding of human group life in our own society and in global perspective.

4. Explain how sociology arose as a new scientific discipline through the work of Auguste Comte, Emile Durkheim, Karl Marx, Harriet Martineau, and other influential nineteenth century social thinkers.

5. Explain the basic assumptions of the structural-functional, social-conflict, and symbolic-interactionist theoretical paradigms.

Key Terms and Concepts

The following terms are important to your understanding of the material presented in this lesson.

global perspective
latent functions
macro-level orientation
manifest functions
micro-level orientation
positivism
social functions
social structure
social-conflict paradigm
sociology
stereotype
structural-functional paradigm
symbolic-interaction paradigm
theory

Term undefined in the text:

sociological imagination – The ability to understand the intersection of history and personal biography, anchored in a social structure.

Video Focus Points

The following points are designed to help you get the most out of the video for this lesson. Read them carefully before viewing the episode.

— Each individual makes choices about how to live his or her life. The video points out how these choices are strongly influenced by the complex web of groups and relationships that we call society.

— Sociologists use the sociological imagination to study how individual concerns and problems reflect larger social issues.

— Individuals can use the understanding that they gain through the study of sociology to better their own lives. As the video shows, children who are raised in poverty and despair may learn how to succeed through educational attainment.

— Sociologists have discovered that poor health, low educational attainment, and other problems are not just the problems of individual people, but that they are related to social factors such as race, ethnicity, and social class.

— Sociology can be used not only to understand society but to change it for the better. Results of sociological research can be used to influence public policy.

Text Focus Points

These are the main points presented in the text assignment for this lesson. Read them carefully before reading the text.

— Sociology looks at human groups in a particular way. The sociological perspective involves a search for patterns of group life, and how society influences the individuals within it.

— It is important to understand the relationship of one's own society to other societies of the world. By adopting a global perspective, sociologists show the interconnectedness of all the world's people. Problems that affect one nation are frequently related to problems affecting other nations as well.

— Sociology in not the same as common sense, which is often inaccurate and contradictory. Sociologists use theory and research to develop an objective understanding of the behavior of human groups.

— French social thinker Auguste Comte was the first to use the term "sociology." While other social thinkers sought to describe society as they thought it should be, sociologists attempt to scientifically understand society as it actually is.

— The three major theoretical paradigms in sociology are the structural-functional paradigm, the social-conflict paradigm, and the symbolic-interaction paradigm. These approaches help sociologists to organize their thinking about how human group life is organized.

Critical Thinking

These activities are designed to help you examine the material in this lesson in greater depth.

1. Sociology teaches us that the decisions we make and the situations in which we find ourselves are strongly influenced by the society in which we live. Does this mean that our lives are, in effect, already planned before we are born because of our social class, race, religion, and other social statuses?

2. How would each of the three major theoretical paradigms (structural-functional, social-conflict, and symbolic-interaction) view the situation of Oralia Bahena, as depicted in the video "Connections," Episode 1?

3. What is unique about the sociological perspective? That is, how does the way that sociologists view their subject matter differ from the view of psychologists or biologists? Do you think that the sociological perspective is more legitimate than the perspective of psychology or biology? Why or why not?

TEST YOUR LEARNING

After answering the following questions, check your responses against the answer key at the end of this book. Review any questions that you answered incorrectly.

Multiple Choice

1. Which of the following decisions typically made by individuals is affected by the cultural and social structural context in which the decision takes place?
   a. Whom to marry
   b. What college to attend
   c. What occupation to pursue

    d. All of these choices

2. When examining human society, sociologists focus most closely on
   a. personality types.
   b. general patterns.
   c. individual biographies.
   d. common sense.

3. French sociologist Emile Durkheim found that suicide rates were lowest among people
   a. currently in their second marriage.
   b. who were most individualistic.
   c. with strong social ties.
   d. who were wealthy.

4. Women in which of the following countries have the fewest children on average?
   a. United States
   b. India
   c. South Africa
   d. Niger

5. Members of minority groups are keenly aware that they are seen as _____ by members of the dominant group.
   a. insiders
   b. outsiders
   c. global citizens
   d. positivists

6. According to the sociological perspective, "we have a say in how we play our cards, but
   a. we can never play a winning hand."
   b. the house always wins."
   c. society deals us the hand."
   d. society does not deal the whole deck."

7. The nineteenth century social thinker who first coined the term "sociology" was
   a. Karl Marx.
   b. Emile Durkheim.
   c. Harriet Martineau.
   d. Auguste Comte.

8. Which of the following statements is congruent with the positivism point of view?
   a. Common sense is nearly always based on truth.
   b. Society is best studied scientifically.
   c. There is no such thing as a sociological law.
   d. Sociologists should remain optimistic about social life.

9. Sociologist C. Wright Mills referred to the ability to see how individual decisions are influenced by the larger society as
   a. the intellectual skill set.
   b. the sociological imagination.
   c. the psychological lens.
   d. the sociological perspective.

10. The fact that only a small percentage of the American population attends the most prestigious universities illustrates which of the following sociological concepts?
    a. Stereotypes
    b. Inequality
    c. The sociological imagination
    d. Positivism

11. Which of the following sociologists is best known for his/her studies of slavery, factory workers, and the rights of women?
    a. Jane Addams
    b. Harriet Martineau
    c. Herbert Spencer
    d. Emile Durkheim

12. A sociologist who suggests that schools perpetuate the inequality found in the wider society is adopting which theoretical paradigm?
    a. Structural-functional
    b. Social-conflict
    c. Symbolic-interaction
    d. Micro-level analysis

Short Answer

13. Discuss the circumstances in which the young Oralia Bahena grew up, and how they influenced the type of life she would have.

14. Use C. Wright Mills' concept of the sociological imagination to explain the problem of unemployment.

15. Compare and contrast the way in which the structural-functional paradigm and the social-conflict paradigm would view the issue of poverty.

Truth Be Told

OVERVIEW

Armed with the framework of the sociological perspective, sociological investigation can begin. The performance of sociological research is a scientific process, and the science of sociology bases its research on *empirical evidence*, meaning facts that can be verified by observation or experience.

Scientific research is based on *concepts*, or mental constructs that represent some part of the world in a simplified form. Measurable indicators of concepts, called *variables*, must be valid and reliable. When they measure what the researcher intends them to measure and not something else, variables are *valid*. They are *reliable* if they give consistent results each time they are administered. By studying the relationships between variables, sociologists are able to draw conclusions about how concepts such as gender and social class relate to each other.

Sociologists search for correlation—a relationship by which two or more variables change together—among variables. The fact that two variables are correlated does not, however, mean that one is the cause of the other. In order to establish causality, three criteria must be satisfied. The variables must be correlated, the cause must come before the effect in time, and there must not be a third variable or spurious factor that influences the variables in a way that makes them vary together.

Three frameworks guide sociological research: the scientific approach, the interpretive approach, and the critical sociology approach. The *scientific approach* to sociology advocates the goal of *objectivity*, or personal neutrality.

Most sociologists agree that complete objectivity is not possible, since sociologists are part of the society that they study, and they have personal biases just like anyone else. German sociologist Max Weber argued that sociology should be *value-free*; that is to say that researchers should avoid having their own biases influence the research they conduct. Sociologists who adopt the scientific framework believe that allowing the facts to speak for themselves to the greatest extent possible is a useful goal. They usually advocate the use of *quantitative* analysis, which involves collection and analysis of numerical data.

The *interpretive* framework goes beyond simply observing behavior to focus on the meanings that people attach to their social behaviors. Interpretive sociologists often make use of *qualitative* analysis, which involves observation and unstructured interviews to reveal how people understand their surroundings.

A third framework for sociological research is *critical sociology*; an approach that explicitly rejects the notion of scientific objectivity and focuses on using research to change society for the better. Critical sociologists often "take sides" and advocate for certain groups, usually those that are relatively powerless and dominated by more powerful groups.

Sociological research begins with a question that the researcher wants to answer. With the question in mind, the sociologist develops a plan for conducting the research using one of four methods of gathering data: experiment, survey, observation, or use of existing sources that have been collected by others. *Experiments* are designed to determine *cause and effect* under tightly controlled conditions in a laboratory or in the field. Subjects are randomly assigned to either the experimental group or the control group. The experimental group is exposed to the independent variable and the control group is not. Measurements are then taken and comparisons made between the two groups to evaluate the effect of the variable.

    Surveys involve research subjects answering a series of questions in an interview or on a questionnaire. This method is useful for providing precise measurements for quantitative data analysis.

    Some research questions lend themselves to the method of *participant observation*, in which the researcher systematically observes people while participating in their activities. This method is illustrated in the video "Truth Be Told" (Episode 2), when sociologist Mitchell Duneier is seen studying homeless persons by working alongside them as they sell books on a New York City street.

    A final method of gathering research data involves the use of *existing sources,* many of which are available on the Internet. Researchers must ensure, however, that the data are accurate and that they are appropriate for the researcher's particular question.

FOCUS YOUR ATTENTION

Assignments

Read the pages indicated for the text assigned by your instructor.

— *Sociology,* 10th Edition, by Macionis. Chapter 2, "Sociological Investigation," pages 26–55.

— *Society: The Basics*, 8th Edition, by Macionis. Chapter 1, "Sociology: Perspective, Theory and Method," pages 15–31.

Watch Episode 2, "Truth Be Told," after scanning the Video Focus Points.

Learning Objectives

After completing your study of this lesson, you should be familiar with the facts and concepts presented and should be able to:

1. Explain what makes sociology a scientific discipline.

2. Compare and contrast the scientific, interpretive, and critical sociology frameworks for research.

3. Explain the four methods of collecting research data: survey, experiment, observation, and existing sources.

4. Discuss some of the factors that influence sociologists' choice of research topics.

5. Explain why sociologists disagree about whether researchers should strive for objectivity in their research.

Key Terms and Concepts

The following terms are important to your understanding of the material presented in this lesson.

cause and effect
concept
correlation
critical sociology
empirical evidence
existing sources (of data)
experiment
interpretive sociology
measurement
objectivity
participant observation
qualitative methods
quantitative methods
reliability
science
scientific sociology
survey
theory
validity
value-free
variable

Term undefined in the text:

ethnography – The research method that involves the study of people first hand by observing them and getting involved in their lives set apart.

Video Focus Points

The following points are designed to help you get the most out of the video for this lesson. Read them carefully before viewing the episode.

— Sociological research begins with a question that is suggested by a particular problem or social issue or by the researcher's personal interest. Some researchers are motivated by the desire to improve society by gathering useful information that may lead to social change.

— Sociology is a social science, but most sociologists agree that complete scientific objectivity is not possible since sociologists are part of the social world that they study.

— Some sociologists take the view that researchers should strive to be as objective as possible in their work. German sociologist Max Weber referred to this as the *value-free* approach. Other sociologists feel that their research should not attempt to be objective, but rather it should be designed to better the situations of exploited persons and groups.

— Research may be qualitative or quantitative, involving observations, surveys, experiments, or analysis of secondary data. The methods that are used in a particular study depend on the questions that are being asked.

Text Focus Points

These are the main points presented in the text assignment for this lesson. Read them carefully before reading the text.

— Concepts are mental constructs that represent some part of the world in a simplified form. Variables are measurable indicators of concepts. Variables are correlated with each other if they change together.

— Sociological research usually falls within one of three frameworks: the scientific approach, the interpretive approach, or the critical sociology

approach. Advocates of these approaches disagree as to whether research should be primarily quantitative or qualitative, and whether objectivity should be a goal.

— Research methods are the design of the research that sociologists carry out. Four methods of collecting research data are the experiment, observation, survey, and use of existing data. The method to be used depends on the question that the researcher is asking.

— Sociology is sometimes accused of simply restating common sense ideas or stereotypes. But common sense and stereotypes are often inaccurate, while sociological research analyzes real-world data in order to discover the truth.

Critical Thinking Questions

These activities are designed to help you examine the material in this lesson in greater depth.

1. If complete objectivity in research is impossible to achieve, does this mean that fair and unbiased research cannot be done? Is all research necessarily biased?

2. A researcher decides to conduct a participant observation study of factory employees who steal company property. What ethical dilemmas might the researcher face?

3. A researcher observes that cities with large police forces also have high rates of crime. What possible spurious variables might have an influence on this apparent relationship?

TEST YOUR LEARNING

After answering the following questions, check your responses against the answer key at the end of this book. Review any questions that you answered incorrectly.

Multiple Choice

1. Sociology is a scientific discipline because
   a. it is based on common sense.
   b. it bases knowledge on empirical evidence.
   c. it is carried out in colleges and universities.
   d. it analyzes existing (secondary) data.

2. Which of the following statements is NOT true?
   a. In the United States, various social rules guide our selection of marriage partners.
   b. The United States is highly stratified in terms of income and wealth.
   c. Definitions of "feminine" and "masculine" change over time across the world.
   d. In most societies, marriage is based on romantic love.

3. Which of the following is defined as "a mental construct that represents some part of the world in a simplified form"?
   a. Concept
   b. Variable
   c. Measurement
   d. Statistic

4. The family, the economy, gender, and social class are examples of
   a. concepts.
   b. variables.
   c. measurements.
   d. correlations.

5. A variable is considered to be _____ if it measures what the researcher intends it to measure and not something else.
   a. valid
   b. reliable
   c. operational
   d. correlational

6. If a variable that measures income is found to change along with a variable that measures educational level, then
   a. income causes educational level.
   b. educational level causes income.
   c. the variables are correlated.
   d. there is no relationship between the variables.

7. In the video "Truth Be Told," we see Professor Mitchell Duneier studying homeless men by working alongside them as they sell books on New York City streets. This method of data collection is known as
   a. an experiment.
   b. a survey.
   c. participant observation.
   d. analysis of existing data.

8. A researcher finds that delinquency rates are high in areas where people live in crowded housing, but both delinquency and living in crowded housing are the result of being poor. Which of the following statements is true?
   a. Delinquency causes people to live in crowded housing.
   b. Living in crowded housing causes delinquency.
   c. The apparent relationship between delinquency and crowded housing is a spurious correlation.
   d. There is no statistical relationship between delinquency, crowded housing, and being poor.

9. French sociologist Emile Durkheim observed that the degree of social integration (the cause) affects the suicide rate (the effect). In this example, suicide rate is
   a. the dependent variable.
   b. the independent variable.
   c. the correlational variable.
   d. the spurious variable.

10. German Sociologist Max Weber stated that researchers should strive to be *value-free* once their research is underway. This means that they should be
    a. precise.
    b. scientific.
    c. objective.
    d. quantitative.

11. Which of the following research frameworks focuses on the need for social change?
    a. The scientific approach
    b. The interpretive approach
    c. The critical sociology approach
    d. The participant observation approach

12. The research method that involves studying people at first hand by observing them and getting involved in their lives is known as
a. critical sociology.
b. scientific sociology.
c. quantitative analysis.
d. ethnography.

Short Answer

13. Explain why a researcher who is studying homeless street people might choose to use participant observation instead of other research methods.

14. Explain what is meant by a spurious correlation.

15. Discuss the viewpoints of the three major research method frameworks (scientific sociology, the interpretive framework, and critical sociology) concerning objectivity in sociological research.

Common Ground

OVERVIEW

The values, beliefs, behavior, and material objects that together form a people's way of life is known as their *culture*. It is what makes us human. Animals are unable to create complex cultures. Through culture, human groups are able to control their environment and adapt to it, as well as to create complicated and enduring social institutions such as family, education, law, government, religion, and the economy. *Society* refers to the people who interact in a defined territory and share a common culture.

Culture makes different groups of people distinctive from each another. Although all human beings are members of a single species—*homo sapiens*—cultural differences abound from one nation to another, and within nations. Culture is becoming increasingly global in nature due to the integration between multinational economies, greater communication and flow of information, and the increased migration of the world's peoples.

All cultures consist of objects and ideas. Material culture is the tangible objects common to a culture ranging from chopsticks to skyscrapers. Nonmaterial culture is composed of symbols, language, values, and norms. *Symbols* are things that are recognized by members of a culture as having a certain meaning. For example, people view flags as strong symbols of national pride and identity.

Language is a system of symbols that allows members of a culture to communicate with each other. Spoken language allows people to communicate in a face-to-face manner. Written language allows communications to be recorded and transmitted. Language reflects the culture of which it is a part, but it also shapes the dimensions of that culture. According to the *Sapir-Whorf hypothesis*, languages provide their speakers with categories of thought.

Values are broad cultural standards of goodness, desirability, and beauty. They generate beliefs, which are statements that people hold to be true. For example, an American cultural value is democracy. This generates people's belief that all citizens over the age of 18 should be able to vote. Sometimes cultural values contradict each other, such as the value of equal opportunity and the contradictory values of racism and group superiority. This illustrates the tension between ideal culture—things as they should be—and real culture—things as they actually are.

Norms are rules and expectations by which a society guides the behavior of its members. They range from relatively trivial folkways to major mores and taboos.

Cultural variation is related to technological development. The culture of hunting and gathering societies, horticultural/pastoral societies, agricultural societies, industrial societies, and postindustrial societies each reflect the technology that is used to produce food and other goods and services. As more sophisticated and pervasive technology appears, cultures become more complex, and greater levels of inequality arise based on the control of surplus wealth. Modern industrial and postindustrial societies contain cultures that are highly diverse or multicultural. Many contain *subcultures* made up of groups whose practices set them apart from the dominant culture. Members of the Pennsylvania Dutch (Amish) subculture hold to their own values and norms while making necessary accommodations to the wider American culture. Countercultures also set themselves apart from mainstream society, arising in opposition to the dominant culture.

Sociologists propose a number of theoretical perspectives in order to explain the role of culture in society and cultural variation. The structural-functional paradigm suggests that culture is built on shared values in response to societal needs. The social-conflict approach looks at ways that cultural practices benefit some groups but not others. The third paradigm employed to explain culture is sociobiology. *Sociobiology* examines the possible influence of biological factors on culture, claiming that certain universal ideas present in almost every culture are a result of man's common biology, and not a social construct. However, critics claim that most studies suggest culture is primarily a social, learned behavior, rather than a biological phenomenon.

Sociologists point out that cultural variations arise over time as groups adapt to their environment. Cultural change can occur within a culture either through the introduction of new technological innovations, the process of discovery, or diffusion. Given the many variations and changes possible, sociologists advocate the practice of *cultural relativism*—the process of evaluating a culture by its own standards rather than by those of the evaluator—when studying another culture. Judging a culture solely by the standards of one's own culture is known as *ethnocentrism*. It is through cultural relativism that we not only learn about other cultures, but develop a better understanding of our own.

FOCUS YOUR ATTENTION

Assignments

Read the pages indicated for the text assigned by your instructor.

— *Sociology*, 10th Edition, by Macionis. Chapter 3, "Culture," pages 56–87.

— *Society: The Basics*, 8th Edition, by Macionis. Chapter 2, "Culture," pages 34–61.

Watch Episode 3, "Common Ground," after scanning the Video Focus Points.

Learning Objectives

After completing your study of this lesson, you should be familiar with the facts and concepts presented and should be able to:

1. Explain the nonmaterial (symbols, values, language, and norms) and material components of culture.

2. Show how members of the Pennsylvania Dutch (Amish) subculture maintain their material and nonmaterial culture while living in the midst of mainstream American culture.

3. Discuss how technology is related to cultural variation in simple and complex societies.

4. Explain the idea of multiculturalism, and the sociological point of view concerning ethnocentrism and cultural relativism.

5. Compare the assumptions of structural-functional theory and social-conflict theory concerning how culture affects individuals, groups, and the wider society.

Key Terms and Concepts

The following terms are important to your understanding of the material presented in this lesson.

counterculture
cultural integration
cultural lag
cultural relativism
cultural transmission
cultural universals
culture
culture shock
ethnocentrism
folkways
high culture
language
material culture
mores

multiculturalism
nonmaterial culture
norms
popular culture
Sapir-Whorf thesis
society
subculture
symbol
values

Terms undefined in the text:

planned obsolescence – The practice of designing a product so that it will become useless or obsolete in a short amount of time, requiring consumers to purchase another product of the same type to replace it.

pluralism – The coexistence of many different cultural groups within one society or nation.

Video Focus Points

The following points are designed to help you get the most out of the video for this lesson. Read them carefully before viewing the episode.

— The United States is a highly pluralistic society that encompasses many different cultural and subcultural groups. American culture tends to be materialistic, consumption-oriented, and tolerant of religious groups.

— The Pennsylvania Dutch (Amish) provide an example of a subculture with values and norms that differ from those of mainstream American culture.

— Amish culture is based on religious ideals and practices, a separate language, and avoidance of modern technology. Materialism is frowned upon. Mainstream American culture is seen as "the outside world" that exists in opposition to Amish ways of life.

— In spite of their subcultural ways, the Amish are part of American culture in many respects. A challenge for the group is how to choose aspects of the mainstream culture that fit with their own values, beliefs, and norms.

Text Focus Points

These are the main points presented in the text assignment for this lesson. Read them carefully before reading the text.

— All humans are members of the same species— *homo sapiens*—but there are wide cultural variations around the globe.

— The components of culture are symbols, language, values and beliefs, and norms. Sometimes there is tension between ideal culture— the way things should be—and real culture— the way things really are.

— Levels of technological sophistication influence a society's culture—hunting/gathering, horticultural/pastoral, agricultural, industrial, or postindustrial.

— Cultural diversity exists across the United States and across the nations of the world. Sociologists avoid ethnocentrism—judging other cultures by the standards of one's own—in favor of cultural relativism—evaluating other cultures by their own standards.

— Sociological theories provide guidelines for thinking about why cultures arise and why they vary. The structural-functional assumes that culture is built on shared values, and that cultural components meet societal needs. The social-conflict approach assumes that culture reflects differences in group power and access to resources.

Critical Thinking Questions

These activities are designed to help you examine the material in this lesson in greater depth.

1. Why do you think cultures differ from each other? Why, for example, do many Americans drive automobiles and many Chinese ride bicycles? Why do women in Iraq cover their faces while American women feel comfortable wearing bikinis?

2. Members of one culture often find foreign cultural practices to be strange and even disturbing. What aspects of mainstream United States culture do followers of traditional Amish ways find unusual, problematic, or upsetting? Why?

3. Explain how the concepts of high culture and popular culture relate to inequality and social class. Give specific examples of each type. Why do you think that members of different social classes participate in different types of high culture or popular culture?

TEST YOUR LEARNING

After answering the following questions, check your responses against the answer key at the end of this book. Review any questions that you answered incorrectly.

Multiple Choice

1. Which of the following is NOT a component of culture?
   a. Symbols
   b. Norms
   c. Instincts
   d. Clothing

2. Which of the following terms is defined as "anything that carries a particular meaning recognized by people who share a culture"?
   a. Cultural universal
   b. Symbol
   c. Belief
   d. Norm

3. The Sapir-Whorf hypothesis suggests that
   a. all languages are basically similar to each other.
   b. languages shape their speakers' views of the world.
   c. American culture is based on the value of competition.
   d. racism is a fundamental American value.

4. Which of the following is NOT one of the core American values identified by sociologist Robin Williams?
   a. Material comfort
   b. Science
   c. Racism and group superiority
   d. Government assistance

5. Many people in the United States favor individual initiative over group conformity. Individualism is
   a. a norm.
   b. a belief.
   c. a symbol.
   d. a value.

6. Most married couples believe that sexual fidelity is important. However studies show that 25 percent of married men and 10 percent of married women report having had sexual relations with other than their spouse. This illustrates which of the following?
   a. Ideal culture versus real culture
   b. Shifting folkways
   c. Cultural diversity
   d. High culture versus popular culture

7. The Pennsylvania Dutch (Amish) are
   a. a counterculture.
   b. a subculture.
   c. culturally diverse.
   d. a global culture.

8. Which of the following is the most monocultural high-income nation of the world?
   a. United States
   b. New Zealand
   c. Germany
   d. Japan

9. Which of the following is the most multicultural of all high-income countries?
   a. United States
   b. Australia
   c. Germany
   d. Japan

10. The difference between a violin and a fiddle is
    a. Violins and fiddles are constructed using different techniques.
    b. Violin bows and fiddle bows are shaped differently.
    c. Violins are generally larger, and therefore louder, than fiddles.
    d. There is no difference between a violin and a fiddle, it is a social creation to distinguish between high and popular culture.

11. Members of traditional Amish communities cease attending school after
    a. third grade.
    b. eighth grade.
    c. graduation from high school.
    d. graduation from college.

12. Which of the following terms is defined as "the practice of judging another culture by the standards of one's own culture"?
    a. Cultural relativism
    b. Multiculturalism
    c. Popular culture
    d. Ethnocentrism

Short Answer

13. The video "Common Ground," Episode 3, reminds us that the American Dream is built on the fundamental American value of individual rights. But for persons who are unemployed, homeless, or living in poverty, the value of individualism can be used by others to blame them for circumstances beyond their control. Explain what this means.

14. An important component of culture is symbols. What are some symbols that are associated with your native country? Do they convey positive or negative images to people in other nations of the world?

15. The textbook contains a map of the Western Hemisphere that appears to be "upside down." Explain why the map appears incorrect to residents of the United States, and what this implies about Americans' view of the world.

Fitting In

OVERVIEW

People do not become fully human unless they experience social interaction from the time they are born. Documented cases of children raised in isolation illustrate how vital social contact is to human development and well-being. Social experience is also the foundation upon which *personality*—an individual's patterns of thinking, feeling, and behaving—is built. *Socialization* is the lifelong social experience by which individuals learn their culture and develop their human potential.

Until the twentieth century, and influenced by Charles Darwin's study of evolution, human behavior was thought to be the product of biology. Psychologist John B. Watson's now generally accepted *behaviorism* theory holds that human behavior is not instinctive, but learned. Which is not to say that biology plays no part in human behavior, but that nurture is of greater importance in shaping human behavior.

Many scholars have studied the process of socialization. Austrian physician Sigmund Freud proposed that the human personality is composed of three parts: the *id* (basic drives), the *ego* (awareness of limitations imposed by society), and the *superego* (conscience). According to Freud, people with fully developed personalities are able to repress their own desires in response to society's demands. Swiss psychologist Jean Piaget suggested that people progress through four stages of cognitive development, with each stage representing a more advanced capacity for abstract, critical thought. Lawrence Kohlberg extended Piaget's

work to focus on the development of moral reasoning. Carol Gilligan criticized Kohlberg for focusing only on male subjects. Her research suggests that men and women use different perspectives when judging morality.

George Herbert Mead developed an influential theory that explains the self as a product of social interaction. Mead proposed that children learn to *take the role of the other* in increasingly complex ways. Erik Erikson pointed to the continuous process of socialization that shapes the human personality throughout the life course.

Socialization occurs whenever interaction takes place, but four social institutions are particularly influential. The *family* has perhaps the greatest impact on the socialization of an individual because of the important learning that takes place in the first years after birth. Parents also provide their children with greater or lesser amounts of cultural capital, which affects success later in life. Children are first exposed to life outside of the home when they enter *school*. Here they learn academic skills as well as the values and norms of the wider society. They also learn how to work within a bureaucratic environment, which trains them for employment in large organizations later on. The *peer group* allows adolescents to express interests and attitudes that may differ from those of their parents. Finally, the *mass media* helps to socialize people by presenting cultural values and norms to a vast audience. No person living in modern society can escape the influence of radio, film, newspapers, magazines, and especially television.

Socialization occurs and changes throughout the life course. American society organizes the life course into four stages: childhood, adolescence, adulthood, and old age. Each stage is part of the lifelong socialization process. *Childhood* is a socially-defined category that allows young persons a period of learning and play. In *adolescence*, teenagers experiment with attitudes and behaviors that are usually different from those of their parents as they prepare for full membership in adult society. *Adulthood* encompasses approximately ages 18 to 65, after which people enter *old age*. American society is highly youth-oriented and personal appearance is very important, which causes difficulties for people as they leave their younger years behind. This fascination with youth can be seen in the popularity of the "Extreme Makeover" television programs, as discussed in the video "Fitting In" (Episode 4).

Certain organizations, such as mental hospitals and prisons, are known as total institutions. They are created in order to resocialize people who cannot function or behave appropriately in society. The process of *resocialization* involves radically changing a person's personality by carefully controlling the environment in which they live and interact with others. Resocialization is accomplished by first breaking down the person's identity, and then building a new self that conforms to the routines and regulations of the institution.

FOCUS YOUR ATTENTION

Assignments

Read the pages indicated for the text assigned by your instructor.

— *Sociology*, 10th edition, by Macionis. Chapter 5, "Socialization," pages 114–137.

— *Society: The Basics*, 8th edition, by Macionis. Chapter 3, "Socialization," pages 62–85.

Watch Episode 4, "Fitting In," after scanning the Video Focus Points.

Learning Objectives

After completing your study of this lesson, you should be familiar with the facts and concepts presented and should be able to:

1. Explain why social interaction is needed in order for people to become fully human.

2. Explain the views of important theorists on how the socialization process takes place.

3. Discuss the role of the following agents of socialization: family, school, peer group, and mass media.

4. Show how the socialization process takes place throughout the life course.

5. Discuss the resocialization process that occurs within total institutions.

Key Terms and Concepts

The following terms are important to your understanding of the material presented in this lesson.

ageism
anticipatory socialization
cohort
concrete operational stage
ego
formal operational stage
generalized other
gerontocracy
gerontology
id
looking-glass self
mass media
peer group
personality
preoperational stage
resocialization
self
sensorimotor stage
significant others
socialization
superego
total institution

Video Focus Points

The following points are designed to help you get the most out of the video for this lesson. Read them carefully before viewing the episode.

— The importance of the socialization process is illustrated by the popularity of reality television shows that offer "extreme makeovers."

— The most important agent of socialization is the family because this is where the bulk of early childhood learning takes place.

— Schools and peer groups are other key agents of socialization.

— Socialization takes place throughout the life course.

Text Focus Points

These are the main points presented in the text assignment for this lesson. Read them carefully before reading the text.

— Children must experience close human interaction in order to become fully human.

— The socialization process allows people to develop personalities and social selves, and to learn the expectations of the culture in which they live.

— Important agents of socialization include the family, the school, peer groups, and the mass media.

— Socialization takes places during each stage of the life course: childhood, adolescence, adulthood, and old age.

— Total institutions such as prisons and mental hospitals use rigid routines and close supervision to accomplish the resocialization of inmates.

Critical Thinking Questions

These activities are designed to help you examine the material in this lesson in greater depth.

1. Research shows that children raised with little or no human contact fail to become fully human. Conversely, do you think that children can be damaged by too much human contact?

2. In what ways, if any, does the average high school resemble a total institution?

3. Through the socialization process, society teaches us how to think, feel, and act. Does this mean that we have no freedom to be ourselves?

TEST YOUR LEARNING

After answering the following questions, check your responses against the answer key at the end of this book. Review any questions that you answered incorrectly.

Multiple Choice

1. When does socialization take place?
   a. Soon after birth
   b. In early childhood
   c. During adolescence
   d. Throughout the life course

2. The cases of Anna and Genie, two children raised in isolation, show that
   a. children need social interaction to become fully human.
   b. children can become fully human without social interaction.
   c. the socialization process is complete by age three.
   d. the importance of parental contact is over-emphasized by researchers.

3. In the famous 1962 study by psychologists Harry and Margaret Harlow, which group of young rhesus monkeys fared the best?
   a. Those raised in complete isolation
   b. Those raised with an artificial mother made of wire mesh
   c. Those raised with an artificial mother made of soft terry cloth
   d. Those raised with an artificial mother filled with warm gel

4. According to Sigmund Freud, which component of the personality is made up of a person's conscious efforts to balance innate pleasure-seeking drives with the demands of society?
   a. Id
   b. Ego
   c. Superego
   d. Eros

5. According to Sigmund Freud, which component of the personality represents the influence of culture in that it forces people to look beyond their own desires?
   a. Id
   b. Ego
   c. Superego
   d. Eros

6. Kate is a one-year-old infant who experiences the world strictly through her senses of sight, smell, touch, taste, and hearing. Which of Jean Piaget's stages of cognitive development is she in?
   a. formal operational stage
   b. concrete operational stage
   c. preoperational stage
   d. sensorimotor stage

7. George Herbert Mead's theory of _____ suggests that we see ourselves as we think others see us.
   a. moral development
   b. the individual self
   c. the looking-glass self
   d. media socialization

8. According to George Herbert Mead, children model their behavior on people—such as parents—who have special importance for socialization. Mead refers to these people as
   a. prestige models.
   b. significant others.
   c. critical others.
   d. significant models.

9. Children first begin to be socialized about gender in
   a. the family.
   b. the school.
   c. the peer group.
   d. the mass media.

10. Young people who experience the world only through sensations of pain and pleasure are in which of Lawrence Kohlberg's stages of moral development?
    a. postconventional stage
    b. conventional stage
    c. preconventional stage
    d. unconventional stage

11. According to George Herbert Mead, people are not able to *take the role of the other* when they are in the _____ stage of development of the self.
    a. generalized other
    b. game
    c. play
    d. imitation

12. Working class families tend to teach their children to be
    a. obedient.
    b. creative.
    c. critical.
    d. nonconformist.

Short Answer

13. What role does the mass media play in defining our views of youth and old age?

14. What do cases of children raised in isolation teach us about the socialization process?

15. How do total institutions accomplish the task of resocialization? Give examples.

Face to Face

OVERVIEW

The process by which people act and react in relation to others—*social interaction*—is also the means by which people construct their social reality. Social structure provides guidelines for people to use in making sense of everyday life. The basic building blocks of social structure are status and roles. *Status* is the social position that a person occupies and is always accompanied by *social roles*, or expected behavior patterns. In other words, people *hold* a status, but they *play* a role.

Status may be *ascribed*, or involuntarily bestowed at birth or later in life Ascribed status includes designations such as daughter, teenager, Cuban, or widower. *Achieved status*, on the other hand, is a social position assumed voluntarily, such as student, athlete, spouse, or truck driver. The status that is most important for a person's identity is referred to as his or her *master status*.

People occupy many statuses at once (their *status set*) and each status requires multiple roles (*role set*) as they interact with others on the basis of their statuses. Difficulties in role performance sometimes lead to *role strain*—tension between roles connected to a single status—and *role conflict*—conflicting roles corresponding to two or more statuses. When a person abandons an important social role—such as when an athlete retires, a member of the clergy leaves the church in favor of a secular life, or a man or woman divorces—he or she has to shed the old role and learn how to interact in the new role, a process sociologists call *role exit*.

The *social construction of reality* is the process by which people creatively shape reality through social interaction. According to the *Thomas theorem*, even situations that are not objectively true can have real consequences if people believe them to be true and act on their shared beliefs.

An individual's reality is constructed from the surrounding culture, based on numerous assumptions and using that culture's rules of everyday interaction. That construction is further influenced by factors as personal as individual interests and extending outward to include local, national, and global events and circumstances. The branch of sociology that examines this process by which people make sense of their everyday surroundings is called *ethnomethodology*.

Dramaturgical analysis views everyday behavior as a dramatic performance in which people are very much like actors putting on performances according to scripts. During their "performance," actors make a claim to a certain social reality that they expect others to support. For example, doctors wear white coats, have diplomas on their office walls, and separate their offices into a front region and a back region. In this way they claim the identity of expert, and show that patients are expected to respect their authority.

People attempt to influence how others see them through the use of language, which carries powerful symbolic meanings. Verbal messages can be supported, enhanced, or contradicted by a speaker's nonverbal communication. Whether intentionally employed or naturally occurring, demeanor, use of space, and body language convey a great deal of information during an individual's *presentation of self*. In order to make social interaction predictable, people cooperate in supporting each other's performances even when they are flawed. By helping each other save face in the wake of an error of performance, everyone is spared embarrassment.

The process of social interaction may be seen in three important dimensions of everyday life: emotions, language, and humor. The emotions that humans display are remarkably consistent across cultures. However, culture influences which events people choose to react to, and how they respond to their emotions and the emotions of others.

Language carries not only surface messages, but hidden meanings as well. As we see in the video "Face to Face" (Episode 5) language can be used to support gender role expectations. For example, words often convey the hidden message that men are more powerful and more socially valuable than women. Language can also be used to persuade others to a certain point of view, as often happens in politics.

Humor allows people to distance themselves from difficult or disturbing situations by providing a safety valve for disturbing sentiments as illustrated by the comedians presented in the video. Humor may also be used to show hostility toward others, such as with ethnic jokes and jokes that cast women in a disparaging light.

Social interaction has significance in even the smallest aspects of daily life. What sociologists often term the mundane of our daily routine can reveal a lot about a culture and the values that it views as important.

FOCUS YOUR ATTENTION

Assignments

Read the pages indicated for the text assigned by your instructor.

— *Sociology*, 10th Edition, by Macionis. Chapter 6, "Social Interaction in Everyday Life," pages 138–161.

— *Society: The Basics*, 8th Edition, by Macionis. Chapter 4, "Social Interaction in Everyday Life," pages 86–107.

Watch Episode 5, "Face to Face," after scanning the Video Focus Points.

Learning Objectives

After completing your study of this lesson, you should be familiar with the facts and concepts presented and should be able to:

1. Explain what social structure is, and how it guides our interaction with others.

2. Explain how statuses and roles act as building blocks of social interaction.

3. Understand how people construct social reality through social interaction.

4. Discuss Erving Goffman's notion of social interaction as a theatrical performance.

5. Show how emotions, language, and humor illustrate the dimensions of everyday life.

Key Terms and Concepts

The following terms are important to your understanding of the material presented in this lesson.

achieved status
ascribed status
dramaturgical analysis
master status
nonverbal communication
personal space
presentation of self
role
role set
role strain
social construction of reality
social interaction
status
status set
Thomas theorem

Terms undefined in the text:

mundane – Ordinary aspects of everyday life.

Sapir-Whorf hypothesis – The view that the languages people speak provide categories of thought that shape the speaker's views of social reality.

Video Focus Points

The following points are designed to help you get the most out of the video for this lesson. Read them carefully before viewing the episode.

— People often use humor in social interaction in order to show that they are able to transcend difficult or disturbing situations.

— The dimensions of social interaction, such as personal space and nonverbal communication, vary from one culture to another.

— Language shapes people's categories of thought and their views of social reality.

— Everyday social interaction consists of people playing the roles that they must play, according to the social status positions they occupy.

— Even the mundane tasks of every day life have a significance in terms of maintaining social interaction and they can tell us a lot about a society's culture and values.

Text Focus Points

These are the main points presented in the text assignment for this lesson. Read them carefully before reading the text.

— Social structure provides the framework for interaction between people.

— The key components of social structure are status and role.

— People construct social reality as they interact with others.

— Social interaction can be viewed as a theatrical performance, where social roles are played in order to make everyday life predictable.

— Emotions, language, and humor are ways that people create social reality and respond to it.

Critical Thinking Questions

These activities are designed to help you examine the material in this lesson in greater depth.

1. If Goffman's notion of interaction as a theatrical performance is accurate, does this mean

that people are acting insincerely as they go about daily life?

2. Why do you think many comedians are members of minority groups?

3. How are master statuses influenced by social norms such as society's view of women?

TEST YOUR LEARNING

After answering the following questions, check your responses against the answer key at the end of this book. Review any questions that you answered incorrectly.

Multiple Choice

1. The basic components of social structure are
   a. prestige and income.
   b. income and status.
   c. status and role.
   d. role and occupation.

2. Chris is a college student during the day and a part-time store clerk in the evening. Each of these social positions require her to perform certain duties and act in certain ways. Sociologists refer to these expected behavior patterns as
   a. statuses.
   b. roles.
   c. institutions.
   d. interactions.

3. Which of the following is an ascribed status?
   a. Student
   b. Mother
   c. Woman
   d. Hockey player

4. _____ is a status that has special importance for social identity, often shaping a person's entire life.
   a. Master role
   b. Status set
   c. Master status
   d. Role set

5. How many roles make up the role set that is attached to a single social status?
   a. One
   b. Three
   c. Ten
   d. Many

6. Monique is a mother who also holds a job outside of the home, a situation she finds difficult and emotionally draining. Her situation illustrates the sociological concept of
   a. role conflict.
   b. role strain.
   c. role inconsistency.
   d. role reversal.

7. Personal space for most Americans is approximately
   a. 6 to 9 inches.
   b. 1 to 1½ feet.
   c. 2 to 3 feet.
   d. 3 to 5 feet.

8. According to the Thomas theorem,
   a. everyday life is similar to actors in a play.
   b. you hold a status but you play a role.
   c. situations that are defined as real are real in their consequences.
   d. situations that are incorrectly defined result in diminished social status.

9. According to Erving Goffman's dramaturgical analysis, a _____ is like a part in a play, and a _____ serves as the script, supplying dialogue and action for the characters.
   a. role, role set
   b. status, status set
   c. role, status
   d. status, role

10. How does the personal space of men and women differ in the United States?
    a. Men claim more personal space than women.
    b. Women claim more personal space than men.
    c. Men and women claim an equal amount of personal space.
    d. No data exist on this issue.

11. Which of the following aspects of emotions is most influenced by biological factors?
    a. Facial expressions used to display emotions
    b. Which situations trigger certain emotions
    c. How people express their emotions in social groups
    d. The value that people place on emotions

12. The influence of gender on language is shown by the word *hysterical*, which comes from the Greek word for
    a. large.
    b. emotions.
    c. uterus.
    d. mother.

Short Answer

13. How does culture influence feelings (emotions)?

14. In what ways do people construct social reality as they interact with others?

15. How is nonverbal communication related to gender roles?

LESSON 6

All Together

OVERVIEW

Human beings seek a sense of belonging. Group membership fills that need, making social groups a key part of every person's life. *Primary groups* such as the family provide expressive support within long-lasting personal relationships. Large *secondary groups* such as work organizations and colleges are impersonal, being organized around a specific task or activity. An important element of group dynamics is leadership. Group leaders may adopt a task-oriented *instrumental* leadership style or a people-oriented *expressive* style. Leaders' decision-making styles may be *authoritarian*, *democratic*, or *laissez-faire*.

Researchers have studied how people conform to group pressure. Solomon Asch's classic experiment shows that people will provide what they know to be a wrong answer when pressured by others. The "electric shock" study conducted by Stanley Milgram, a former student of Asch, suggests that people will obey the orders of authority figures even when their actions may harm others. Group pressure within an organization can lead to *groupthink*, a process wherein individuals feel compelled to silence their own opinions in order to conform to the decision of the group. The video "All Together" (Episode 6) provides an illustration of the sometimes tragic consequences of group think in its discussion of the NASA space shuttle disasters of 1986 and 2003.

People identify with members of their *in-groups*, and feel a sense of opposition to those in their *out-groups*. *Reference groups* provide people with a comparison against which to measure their decisions and evaluations. It is not necessary to belong to a particular group to consider it a reference group.

Formal organizations are large secondary groups organized to achieve their goals efficiently. According to Amitai Etzioni, they may be *utilitarian* organizations (task oriented), *normative* organizations/voluntary associations (issue-oriented), or *coercive* organizations (punishment- or treatment-oriented). Many modern organizations are bureaucracies, with individuals performing specialized tasks in a routinized manner within a formal and hierarchical organizational structure. Bureaucracy is highly efficient, but may produce worker alienation and increased distance between managers and workers.

Two competing models of work organization have emerged in the past century. In the early 1900s Frederick Winslow Taylor proposed a model of *scientific management* in which the primary goal is efficiency through routinization of tasks. Taylor's model reached a high point in the automobile assembly lines of Henry Ford and others. In contrast to Taylor's model, beginning in the 1980s, the Japanese model became highly influential for American organizations. The Japanese model stresses teamwork, community, and shared decision-making.

These two models compete to this day for acceptance in American organizations. The overall success of Taylor's model resulted in greater routinization in all types of work environments, leading to a process that sociologists refer to as "McDonaldization," which is named after the highly routinized system that made the fast food chain such a success. As work organizations have increased their levels of efficiency, predictability, standardization, and automation, much of American life has become McDonaldized. However, some organizations have adapted to the changing nature of work in American society by becoming more flexible and open. Such organizations have fewer levels of hierarchy and an increased emphasis on teamwork. This new model fits well in the post-industrial work environment that is based on creation and dissemination of information rather than on the production of specific industrial commodities.

Lastly, as we see in the video's look at the Outward Bound program, every organization has its own unique culture that is linked to the values and norms of the wider society.

FOCUS YOUR ATTENTION

Assignments

Read the pages indicated for the text assigned by your instructor.

— *Sociology*, 10th edition, by Macionis. Chapter 7, "Groups and Organizations," pages 162–187.

— *Society: The Basics*, 8th edition, by Macionis. Chapter 5, "Groups and Organizations," pages 108–133.

Watch Episode 6, "All Together," after scanning the Video Focus Points.

Learning Objectives

After completing your study of this lesson, you should be familiar with the facts and concepts presented and should be able to:

1. Understand the nature of social groups and how they are influenced by leadership styles, number of members, social diversity (race, class, and gender), and pressures to conform such as groupthink.

2. Understand the nature and types of formal organizations.

3. Explain what bureaucracy is and why it is important in modern society.

4. Illustrate the differences between the scientific management model and alternative models.

5. Critically evaluate benefits and problems associated with the McDonaldization of society.

Key Terms and Concepts

The following terms are important to your understanding of the material presented in this lesson.

bureaucracy
bureaucratic inertia
bureaucratic ritualism
category
expressive leadership
formal organization
groupthink
in-group
instrumental leadership
network
oligarchy
out-group
primary group
rationality
rationalization of society
reference group
scientific management
secondary group
social group
tradition

Video Focus Points

The following points are designed to help you get the most out of the video for this lesson. Read them carefully before viewing the episode.

— Primary groups provide expressive support and a strong sense of community.

— Groups can exert pressure on their members to conform, which can lead to groupthink, where individuals de-emphasize their own opinions to conform to the decision of the group. Groupthink can lead to unforeseen and disastrous outcomes such as the space shuttle disasters of 1986 and 2003.

— Large organizations are structured to accomplish complex tasks efficiently.

— Frederick Winslow Taylor's scientific management model was very efficient but it led to worker alienation and increased distance between workers and managers.

— After World War II, the Japanese model of teamwork and worker participation in decision-making became increasingly influential in the United States.

— The prevalence and success of scientific management in industrial production has led to the McDonaldization of much of American society.

— Increased global competition and the shift from an industrial to an information-based post-industrial economy has led many organizations to see their employees as a valuable resource and to focus more on teamwork.

Text Focus Points

These are the main points presented in the text assignment for this lesson. Read them carefully before reading the text.

— People live most of their lives within social groups.

— Primary groups offer expressive support while secondary groups accomplish instrumental tasks.

— Pressure to conform to the opinions of a group rather than defending one's individual judgment can lead to groupthink, which can be very detrimental to an organization.

— Formal organizations are large secondary groups created to achieve tasks efficiently.

— Bureaucratic organizations are particularly important in modern society.

— The scientific management model of work organization has been challenged by alternatives such as the Japanese model.

— An adaptation of the scientific management model is called "McDonaldization," which is the routinization of all aspects of American society in the name of greater efficiency, consistency, and automation. Many are concerned that the increased McDonaldization of society is dehumanizing and limits our freedom.

— Increased global competition and the shift from an industrial to an information-based post-industrial economy has led many organizations to become more open, flexible, less hierarchical, and more team-oriented.

Critical Thinking Questions

These activities are designed to help you examine the material in this lesson in greater depth.

1. What do the results of research by Asch, Milgram, and Janis imply about the social causes of group conformity? Does their research mean that people always risk making misguided decisions in group situations?

2. Why has the Japanese model of group organization been such an important influence on American manufacturing?

3. On the whole, do you think the bureaucratic form of group organization is good for society or bad for society? Why?

TEST YOUR LEARNING

After answering the following questions, check your responses against the answer key at the end of this book. Review any questions that you answered incorrectly.

Multiple Choice

1. Students sitting in a large lecture hall are an example of a
   a. group.
   b. category.
   c. crowd.
   d. formal organization.

2. A married couple, a family, and a circle of friends are examples of
   a. groups.
   b. categories.
   c. crowds.
   d. formal organizations.

3. Luis and Mark are close friends. According to Charles Horton Cooley's classification, together they form a(n)
   a. primary group.
   b. secondary group.
   c. formal organization.
   d. out-group.

4. Members of a(n) _____ define each other primarily according to who they are, rather than according to what tasks they can perform.
   a. primary group
   b. secondary group
   c. formal organization
   d. out-group

5. Which of the following types of leadership is least effective in promoting group goals?
   a. Authoritarian leadership
   b. Democratic leadership
   c. Laissez-faire leadership
   d. All of the above are equally effective in promoting group goals

6. What conclusion may be drawn from the results of Stanley Milgram's "electric shock" experiment?
   a. Most people actively resist the orders given by authority figures.
   b. Most people follow the orders given by authority figures.
   c. Democratic leadership is more effective than authoritarian leadership.
   d. Soldiers are more satisfied in units where promotion to higher rank is common.

7. Irving Janis noted that group members sometimes conform to the wishes of the group rather than insisting on their own point of view, a process he referred to as
   a. a reference group.
   b. groupthink.
   c. peer pressure.
   d. uniformity.

8. According to Georg Simmel, a group with _____ members is fundamentally different from groups of other sizes.
   a. two
   b. three
   c. four
   d. seven

9. In contrast to the scientific management model of work organization, the Japanese model is based on
   a. bureaucracy.
   b. specialization.
   c. hierarchy.
   d. teamwork.

10. According to Peter Blau, the larger a social group is, the more likely its members are to
    a. interact with persons outside the group.
    b. interact with persons inside the group.
    c. define out-group members in positive terms.
    d. have few social networks.

11. According to the video "All Together" (Episode 6), adventure groups such as Outward Bound explicitly strive to teach participants the value of
    a. hierarchy.
    b. authority.
    c. community.
    d. individualism.

12. According to Robert Michel's *Iron Law of Oligarchy*, in a bureaucracy
    a. the few will rule the many.
    b. the many will rule the few.
    c. democratic organization is the most efficient type.
    d. organizational officials are close to the public.

Short Answer

13. What is the primary advantage of Tayloristic scientific management?

14. What is the difference between a social group and a category? Give an example of each.

15. Discuss the nature of primary groups, secondary groups, reference groups, in-groups, out-groups, and social networks.

LESSON 7

Against the Grain

OVERVIEW

Deviance is a definition applied by society to various acts and attitudes that it views as unacceptable or undesirable. It is the recognized violation of cultural norms, ranging from relatively mild violations such as traffic offenses to serious transgressions such as murder. When the norm violated is a criminal law, the deviance is termed a *crime*. Sociologists point out that no act is inherently deviant. Even killing another human being is allowed under certain circumstances such as self-defense or war. Deviance casts the violator as somehow different from others; an outsider.

Social control is society's attempt to regulate the thought and behavior of its population in order to ensure that most of the people follow the norms most of the time. Informal social control is carried out in everyday life by the people with whom one interacts. A parent's words of praise, or the taunts of peers directed at a child who is dressed in an unusual manner are examples of informal controls. Serious deviant behavior arouses formal social control through the *criminal justice system*, which consists of police, the courts, and systems of punishment including jails and prisons.

Theories of deviance attempt to explain why it occurs, and how levels of deviance vary. Biological and personality theories may explain some types of deviant behavior, but sociologists view deviance primarily as an outgrowth of the way that society is organized, not as a characteristic of the person who commits the act. Sociological theories of deviance are related to the three major theoretical paradigms: structural-

functional, symbolic-interaction, and social-conflict.

Structural-functional explanations assume that deviance is an inherent characteristic of society—that there can be no society without norm violations of some sort. This is because deviance is viewed as functional for society. The deviant actions of a few clarify the boundaries of acceptable behavior for the many. Deviance can also draw members of a group together in response to a common threat. Robert Merton's strain theory suggests that when society does not provide sufficient legal means of achieving success, some people will be pushed to engage in disapproved or illegal means of achieving culturally-accepted goals. Other theories in the structural-functional tradition focus on subcultures whose values and norms support the involvement of their members in deviant activities.

Labeling theory is an outgrowth of the symbolic-interaction theoretical paradigm. It assumes that all members of society engage in brief and transitory acts of deviance (primary deviance). However, deviance is more likely to continue (secondary deviance) if others become aware of the deviance and respond to it by stigmatizing the offender. Other approaches in the symbolic-interaction tradition include differential association theory and control theory. Differential association theory assumes that deviance is learned within peer groups such as youth gangs, and control theory suggests that deviance is less likely if people have stronger bonds and involvement with conventional society.

29

Social-conflict theories of deviance examine the role of inequality and power differences. Laws are viewed as definitions created by powerful groups in order to keep groups with less power from becoming a threat to their privileged positions. According to the conflict approach, laws reflect the struggle between rich and poor social classes. Conflict theorists have focused attention on deviance by privileged persons, including *white-collar crime, corporate crime,* and *organized crime.*

The violation of criminal law includes crimes against persons (violent crime), crimes against property (property crime), and *hate crimes* (criminal acts motivated by racial or other bias against the victim). Statistics collected by the Federal Bureau of Investigation (FBI) indicate that the perpetrator of a given crime will most likely conform to a predictable profile based on age, race, and sex. Crime statistics also indicate that even though crime rates have been declining in recent years, the United States has one of the highest rates of violent crime among the world's developed nations.

Social control of crime occurs within the criminal justice system. Police enforce the laws by investigating criminal acts and bringing alleged offenders into custody. The courts determine whether the alleged offender is guilty of the offense, and what the punishment will be. Punishment has several goals, including *retribution, deterrence, rehabilitation,* and *societal protection.* Jails and prisons often do not rehabilitate criminal offenders. Programs like Delancey Street, shown in the video, may provide an effective means of assisting former criminals to become productive members of mainstream society.

FOCUS YOUR ATTENTION

Assignments

Read the pages indicated for the text assigned by your instructor.

— *Sociology,* 10th Edition, by Macionis. Chapter 8, "Deviance," pages 188–219.

— *Society: The Basics,* 8th Edition, by Macionis. Chapter 7, "Deviance," pages 160–189.

Watch Episode 7, "Against the Grain," after scanning the Video Focus Points.

Learning Objectives

After completing your study of this lesson, you should be familiar with the facts and concepts presented and should be able to:

1. Explain what sociologists mean when they say that no act is inherently deviant.

2. Discuss the basic assumptions and implications of structural-functional, symbolic-interaction, and social-conflict theories of deviance.

3. Explain the nature of crime and the types of crime. Discuss the implications of criminal statistics for showing variations in the levels of criminal behavior.

4. Outline the structure of the criminal justice system, and explain the role that each part plays in the social control of crime.

Key Terms and Concepts

The following terms are important to your understanding of the material presented in this lesson.

corporate crime
crime
crimes against property (property crimes)
crimes against the person (violent crimes)
criminal justice system
criminal recidivism
deterrence
deviance
hate crime
organized crime
plea bargaining
rehabilitation
retribution
social control
societal protection
stigma
victimless crimes
white-collar crime

Video Focus Points

The following points are designed to help you get the most out of the video for this lesson. Read them carefully before viewing the episode.

— Definitions of deviance vary from time to time and from place to place. An example is the changing views of drinking and drug use in the United States during the past one hundred years.

— Types of crime include violent crimes and property crimes. Some people suggest that hate crimes—offenses directed at victims because of the victim's personal characteristics—should be placed in a unique and separate category.

— Drugs are a significant problem in the United States. Some people suggest that the government's War on Drugs has discriminated against minorities.

— Jails and prisons often do not provide offenders with the skills and motivation to rehabilitate and rejoin mainstream society. Organizations such as the Delancey Street Foundation may offer a model for successful rehabilitation programs.

Text Focus Points

These are the main points presented in the text assignment for this lesson. Read them carefully before reading the text.

— Deviance is the recognized violation of cultural norms, ranging from mild to serious. Society determines how deviance is defined, what acts or attributes are considered deviant, who is deviant, and how norm violations are treated.

— The creation of social norms, and the means by which they are enforced (social control) are related to inequality. Powerful people have the power to use the law to protect their interests.

— Sociological theories of deviance attempt to explain why deviance and crime occur. The various theories are related to the three major sociological theoretical paradigms: structural-functional, symbolic-interaction, and social-conflict.

— Crime is the violation of criminal laws enacted by a locality, state, or the federal government. The two major types of crime are crimes against the person and crimes against property.

— Social control of crime is carried out by the criminal justice system, which is made up of the police, courts, and punishment.

Critical Thinking Questions

These activities are designed to help you examine the material in this lesson in greater depth.

1. Sociologists assume that deviance results from the ways that society is organized, and the social definitions applied to the violation of social norms. What are the implications of this approach for free will and individual choice?

2. According to the structural-functional approach, deviance is functional. Explain how it is possible that deviance can have positive consequences for society. Does this mean that crime can sometimes be a good thing?

3. As seen in the video "Against the Grain," Episode 7, hate crimes are committed because of the victim's race, religion, ethnicity, sexual orientation, gender, disability status, or other attribute. Is the concept of hate crimes useful, or are hate crimes the same as other forms of deviance?

TEST YOUR LEARNING

After answering the following questions, check your responses against the answer key at the end of this book. Review any questions that you answered incorrectly.

Multiple Choice

1. Which of the following acts is defined as deviant in every known society of the world?
   a. Killing another person
   b. Using property that is not one's own
   c. Questioning the authority of public officials
   d. None of the above

2. Attempts by society to regulate people's thoughts and behavior are referred to by sociologists as
   a. punishment.
   b. mind games.
   c. social conformity.
   d. social control.

3. Which of the following is NOT one of the three social foundations of deviance?
   a. Deviance varies according to cultural norms.
   b. Deviance is a matter of personal choice.
   c. People become deviant because others define them that way.
   d. Both cultural norms and the way people define them involve social power.

4. According to _____, no society can exist without deviance.
   a. Karl Marx
   b. Auguste Comte
   c. Emile Durkheim
   d. Herbert Spencer

5. Which of the following is NOT one of the functions of deviance identified by Emile Durkheim?
   a. Deviance prevents social change.
   b. A response to deviance clarifies moral boundaries.
   c. Deviance affirms cultural values and norms.
   d. A response to deviance brings people together.

6. According to Robert Merton's strain theory, homeless street people who reject cultural goals and the approved means of achieving them would be classified as
   a. conformists.
   b. innovators.
   c. ritualists.
   d. retreatists.

7. A basic assumption of labeling theory is
   a. deviance is functional for society.
   b. all people commit some deviant acts during their lives.
   c. definitions of deviance reflect the views of powerful groups.
   d. deviance is learned in intimate primary groups.

8. Referring to alcoholism as a disease is an example of
   a. primary deviance.
   b. secondary deviance.
   c. medicalization of deviance.
   d. institutionalization of deviance.

9. According to the video "Against the Grain" (Episode 7), a primary mission of the Delancey Street Foundation is
   a. holding religious services in nursing homes.
   b. finding a cure for muscular dystrophy.
   c. providing shelter for homeless inner city residents.
   d. helping former deviants to rejoin mainstream society.

10. A basic assumption of Edwin Sutherland's differential association theory is
    a. deviance is learned in groups.
    b. deviance occurs in all societies of the world.
    c. crime is an individual choice.
    d. gangs rarely engage in violent activities.

11. A young man is beaten by a group of teenagers because they believe he is a homosexual. This is an example of
    a. primary deviance.
    b. ritualism.
    c. a crime of passion.
    d. a hate crime.

12. According to the video "Against the Grain" (Episode 7), the U.S. War on Drugs has resulted in a disproportionately high rate of incarceration of
    a. African Americans.
    b. Japanese Americans.
    c. White Ethnic Americans.
    d. Arab Americans.

Short Answer

13. One of the goals of punishment is to rehabilitate offenders. What are some implications of the Delancey Street program for new ways of structuring prison rehabilitation programs?

14. Sociologists assume that no act is inherently deviant. Explain what this statement means. Give specific examples.

15. How are the concepts of power and inequality related to what acts are defined as deviant and which persons are defined as deviant?

Matters of the Flesh

OVERVIEW

Sociologically speaking, human sexuality is of interest in terms of patterns of sexual behavior, from the ways societies define sex to the diversity of individual expression. *Sex* is the biological assignment of a person as male or female based on the number and type of chromosomes inherited from the parents. *Sexuality* refers to how people express themselves sexually. Although sexuality has a biological dimension, sociologists focus on cultural variations in sexual definitions and behavior. The ways that people express themselves sexually are highly variable from one culture to another, and from one time period to another within cultures. This indicates that human sexual behavior is not instinctual, as it is with nonhuman animals.

Throughout American history, attitudes toward sexuality have been quite restrictive. Some relaxation occurred during the Roaring Twenties (1920s) and again during the sexual revolution of the 1960s. Since the invention of the oral contraceptive ("the pill") in 1960 and legalization of abortion in 1973, American women, both married and unmarried, have experienced greater freedom to participate in sexually active lifestyles. This freedom has been tempered by the threat of sexually transmitted diseases such as HIV/AIDS, and by the resurgence of a sexual counterrevolution emphasizing family values and sexual responsibility.

Today, the United States is a society that is both restrictive and permissive with regard to sexuality. Sexuality is pervasive in our culture and mass media, but the controversy surrounding sexuality education in schools that is depicted in the video "Matters of the Flesh" (Episode 8), clearly shows the prevalence of a restrictive attitude toward sexuality.

Sex and sexuality are related to a number of controversial issues, including teen pregnancy, pornography, prostitution, and sexual violence. Rates of teen pregnancy are high, despite the fact that sexuality education programs exist in most schools. *Pornography* is viewed as exploitive by some, while others argue that it should be protected as an expression of free speech. *Prostitution* is sometimes viewed as a "victimless crime," but many sex workers are poor and some are the victims of abuse. Rape and date rape are examples of sexual violence. Official crime statistics underestimate the extent of rape—which is widespread in the United States—because many incidents are not reported to the police.

Little research has been conducted on sexuality until relatively recently. The first major study, the Kinsey Report released in 1948, generated a great deal of controversy simply because scientists were studying sexual behavior. A major 1994 study by Laumann and his associates revealed the changing social norms concerning sexuality and sexual behavior in American culture.

One aspect of sexuality that researchers are currently studying is the origin of sexual orientation. *Sexual orientation* is a person's romantic and emotional attraction to another person. Sociologists view sexual orientation as a continuum ranging from exclusively *heterosexual* to exclusively *homosexual*. People who are attracted to both sexes are *bisexual*, and those that are not attracted to persons of either sex are termed *asexual*. Some researchers argue that sexual orientation is biologically determined, while others suggest that it is a product of society.

According to structural-functional analysis, sexual behavior must be regulated in order to protect social roles within the family. Symbolic-interaction analysis shows that definitions of sexuality are socially constructed. Social-conflict analysis emphasizes the role that sexuality plays in maintaining the patterns of social inequality found in the larger society.

FOCUS YOUR ATTENTION

Assignments

Read the pages indicated for the text assigned by your instructor.

— *Sociology*, 10th edition, by Macionis. Chapter 9, "Sexuality," pages 220–244.

— *Society: The Basics*, 8th edition, by Macionis. Chapter 6, "Sexuality and Society," pages 134–159.

Watch Episode 8, "Matters of the Flesh," after scanning the Video Focus Points.

Learning Objectives

After completing your study of this lesson, you should be familiar with the facts and concepts presented and should be able to:

1. Explain the biological and cultural aspects of sexuality.

2. Discuss changing attitudes toward sexuality in the United States over the past hundred years.

3. Explain the nature of sexual orientation as a social and biological product.

4. Discuss the dimensions of the controversies over sexuality education, teen pregnancy, pornography, prostitution, and sexual violence and abuse.

5. Outline the basic explanations of sexuality put forth by structural-functional, social-conflict, and symbolic-interaction analysis.

Key Terms and Concepts

The following terms are important to your understanding of the material presented in this lesson.

abortion
asexuality
bisexuality
extramarital sex
hermaphrodite
heterosexism
heterosexuality
homophobia
homosexuality
incest taboo
pornography
premarital sex
primary sex characteristics
prostitution
queer theory
secondary sex characteristics
sex
sexual orientation
sexuality
transsexuals

Video Focus Points

The following points are designed to help you get the most out of the video for this lesson. Read them carefully before viewing the episode.

— Education about sexuality is a controversial issue in America's schools.

— Educators are concerned that sexuality education in the schools be objective and free from religious or political bias.

— Attitudes toward sexuality education mirror attitudes about sexuality in the wider American society.

— Sexuality education struggles to deal with controversial issues in American society such as sexual orientation, abortion, pornography, and sexual abuse.

Text Focus Points

These are the main points presented in the text assignment for this lesson. Read them carefully before reading the text.

— Sexuality is based in biological fact, but the way that it is dealt with is a cultural issue.

— American attitudes toward sexuality have changed from one time period to another.

— The sexual revolution of the 1960s led to changes in attitudes toward premarital sex, abortion, extramarital sex, and homosexuality.

— Controversial sexual issues include teen pregnancy, pornography, prostitution, and sexual violence and abuse.

— Structural-functional analysis suggests that sexuality is important to a smoothly-running society. Symbolic-interaction analysis highlights changing definitions of sexuality as a social construction. Social-conflict analysis points to the role of sexuality in maintaining the inequalities seen in society at large.

Critical Thinking Questions

These activities are designed to help you examine the material in this lesson in greater depth.

1. Why do you think sexuality education in schools is such a controversial subject?

2. Some sociologists have suggested that asking why people are gay is a homophobic question, and that it discriminates against homosexuals. Do you believe that this is true?

3. One hundred years ago, social norms dictated that American women should be virgins at the time of their marriage. Why does society no longer expect this?

TEST YOUR LEARNING

After answering the following questions, check your responses against the answer key at the end of this book. Review any questions that you answered incorrectly.

Multiple Choice

1. Because sexuality is a controversial topic, few researchers conducted studies on it until
   a. the mid nineteenth century.
   b. the early twentieth century.
   c. the mid twentieth century.
   d. the early twenty-first century.

2. The biological distinction between females and males is referred to as
   a. sex.
   b. sexuality.
   c. sexual orientation.
   d. sexual inequality.

3. Which of the following is a primary sex characteristic of females?
   a. Genitals
   b. Wider hips
   c. Body hair
   d. Breasts

4. People with some combination of male and female genitalia are referred to as
   a. homosexuals.
   b. transsexuals.
   c. bisexuals.
   d. hermaphrodites.

5. Which of the following cultural aspects of sexuality is the norm in every one of the world's societies?
   a. Kissing
   b. No intercourse before marriage
   c. The incest taboo
   d. The missionary position

6. Alfred Kinsey and his associates published the first major study of sexuality in the United States in
   a. 1918.
   b. 1948.
   c. 1978.
   d. 1998.

7. According to the textbook, what was the main reason that the Kinsey report was so controversial?
   a. Because of what it said about sexual behavior
   b. Because it showed that scientists were studying sexuality
   c. Because it was conducted by medical doctors
   d. Because it was approved by major religious denominations

8. According to the video "Matters of the Flesh" (Episode 8), why did Renee Walker object to the sexuality education program at her son's school?
   a. She believed that sexuality issues should not be taught in public schools.
   b. She believed that sexuality education encourages young people to engage in sexual activity.
   c. She believed that her religious ideals were not being presented fairly to the students.
   d. She believed that the sexuality education program was biased.

9. After World War II the attitudes of many Americans toward sexuality changed radically. This period of change is often referred to as
   a. the watershed of sexuality.
   b. the sexual revolution.
   c. sexual anomie.
   d. the culture of sex.

10. The oral contraceptive known as "the pill" first became available in the United States in what year?
    a. 1920
    b. 1940
    c. 1960
    d. 1980

11. In the 1980s, there was a widespread movement to limit American's sexual freedom in favor of "family values" and increased sexual responsibility. This movement has been referred to as
    a. Luddism.
    b. the sexual counterrevolution.
    c. the sexual renaissance.
    d. representative sexual democracy.

12. Societal attitudes toward sexuality go through cycles of repression and permissiveness. What was the prevailing attitude in Britain during the reign of Queen Victoria?
    a. Very repressive
    b. Somewhat repressive
    c. Somewhat permissive
    d. Very permissive

Short Answer

13. What changes occurred in American's views of sexuality during the years of the sexual revolution?

14. To what extent is sexuality biological in origin, and to what extent is it a product of society?

15. What social functions does the incest taboo serve for the smooth running of the family and the wider society?

LESSON 9

Ups and Downs

OVERVIEW

All societies distribute scarce resources unequally. *Social stratification* refers to systems that rank categories of people in a hierarchy, and is part of the way that societies are organized, not primarily the result of the talents or efforts of individuals. Although some people can achieve *social mobility*, which is a change in their position in the social hierarchy, most remain at about the same social level as their parents. This is especially true in *caste systems,* such as exists in India, where social standing is based solely on ascribed statuses conferred at birth. Social mobility is more common in *class systems*, such as exists in the United States, where social standing is based on individual achievement as well as ascribed statuses. The former Soviet Union is an example of a society that has attempted in theory to rid itself of stratification to become a classless society, but has not achieved this ideal in practice.

Social stratification systems are supported by ideology—cultural beliefs that justify particular social arrangements, including patterns of inequality. Ideological beliefs are very powerful and can lead people to accept their lot in life, however elevated or low, making it very difficult to change social stratification systems.

Sociological theories attempt to explain why stratification systems exist in societies. The *Davis-Moore thesis* is based on the structural-functionalist assumption that social inequality is beneficial for society as a whole. Some tasks (jobs) are more important than others; therefore people who perform them receive greater rewards of income, prestige, power, or leisure. This, in turn, encourages

people to undergo the training needed to perform important tasks.

Conflict theory, on the other hand, suggests that social stratification benefits some persons and groups at the expense of others. Nineteenth century social thinker Karl Marx suggested that capitalist societies are divided into two classes—the *bourgeoisie* and the *proletariat*—based on ownership of property. Wealthy capitalist property owners are able to control and exploit the propertyless worker class. Marx believed that this situation would eventually become intolerable to the workers, who would rise up and overthrow the capitalists through revolutionary change. Max Weber expanded on Marx's ideas to include not just social class but also status and power.

The amount of inequality in a society depends on its level of technological development. In hunting-and-gathering societies, people are equal because they all perform the same tasks. Inequality increases in horticultural/pastoral and agrarian societies because surpluses can be controlled by a small number of powerful persons and groups. Inequality is high in industrial societies, but it lessens somewhat as legal status grants people greater equality. In postindustrial societies inequality once again increases.

The United States—a post-industrial society—is highly stratified. The richest one percent of families in the United States controls 40 percent of the nation's private wealth. The poorest 40 percent of families have virtually no material wealth. The United States is a class system, where social mobility is widely believed to be possible (the American

37

Dream). As we see in the video "Ups and Downs" (Episode 9), immigrants to America are sometimes able to become successful by owning and operating their own businesses. However, research shows that most people are able to make only modest gains in their class position, usually moving within one class rather than across classes. Mobility is more difficult for some groups, especially minorities and women. For instance, for a long time financial institutions engaged in the illegal practice of "red-lining"—refusing real estate loans to applicants from poor and minority neighborhoods. Many people in America work multiple part-time jobs for low pay. Changes in the global economic structure have caused many employers to move jobs out of the United States to countries where labor costs are lower.

Millions of United States residents live in poverty. The problem is most pronounced among the elderly, racial and ethnic minority groups, women who head households, and children. Up to half a million persons may be homeless at some point during a given year. Millions of people are unable to find jobs that provide them and their families with the necessities of life. Research suggests that the "blame the victim" explanation of poverty is less accurate than the "blame society" approach. However, the ideology of individuality that drives American culture places the blame for poverty on the poor themselves. Welfare programs are controversial for this reason. People in other industrialized nations such as Sweden and Germany are much more likely to view the causes of poverty as a function of social injustices rather than as a reflection of the personal characteristics of the poor.

FOCUS YOUR ATTENTION

Assignments

Read the pages indicated for the text assigned by your instructor.

— *Sociology,* 10th Edition, by Macionis. Chapter 10, "Social Stratification," pages 246–269 and Chapter 11 "Social Class in the United States," pages 270–297.

— *Society: The Basics,* 8th Edition, by Macionis. Chapter 8, "Social Stratification," pages 190–223.

Watch Episode 9, "Ups and Downs," after scanning the Video Focus Points.

Learning Objectives

After completing your study of this lesson, you should be familiar with the facts and concepts presented and should be able to:

1. Explain what social stratification is, and how stratification is structured in the United States and throughout the world.

2. Compare and contrast the Davis-Moore (functionalist) explanation of inequality with Karl Marx's (conflict) explanation.

3. Explain how the amount of social stratification is related to a society's level of technological development.

4. Discuss social class and social mobility in the United States, and how they are related to gender and minority group status.

5. Discuss the issue of poverty in the United States, and why it exists.

Key Terms and Concepts

The following terms are important to your understanding of the material presented in this lesson.

absolute poverty
bourgeoisie
capitalists
caste system
class system
Davis-Moore thesis
feminization of poverty
ideology
income
Kuznets curve
meritocracy
occupational prestige
proletarians
relative poverty
social mobility
social stratification
socioeconomic status (SES)
wealth

Term undefined in the text:

sharecropping – An agrarian system practiced primarily in the southern United States from the post-Civil War era until the middle of the twentieth century. In this system of farming a tenant farmer is provided with the land, seed, and tools to farm a piece of land for the landowner. The tenant farmer receives an agreed upon share of the overall value of the crops produced from which he must deduct the cost of the seed and tools he received from the landowner to work the land.

Video Focus Points

The following points are designed to help you get the most out of the video for this lesson. Read them carefully before viewing the episode.

— Despite the existence of widespread poverty, the United States is seen by many as a land of opportunity where it is possible to better oneself through hard work and educational attainment.

— Americans like to think of their country as a classless society, but there is a wide gap between the richest and poorest Americans.

— Minority group members are particularly at risk for poverty and downward social mobility.

— Many persons who live in poverty hold jobs that offer low pay and few if any fringe benefits such as health insurance. Members of the working poor face a continual risk of financial disaster.

Text Focus Points

These are the main points presented in the text assignment for this lesson. Read them carefully before reading the text.

— Social stratification exists in every society, reflecting the structure of society rather than individual differences.

— Systems of stratification can be classified as open (class system) or closed (caste system).

— The Davis-Moore thesis suggests that stratification is useful for society. Karl Marx's conflict-focused view suggests that powerful persons and groups try to maintain their privileged positions at the expense of the relatively powerless.

Max Weber expanded on Marx's ideas, including status and power with class to explain stratification.

— The amount of inequality in a society depends on the society's level of technological development.

— The United States is a class system with widespread inequality and poverty.

— Minority group members are more likely than whites to experience barriers to upward social mobility.

Critical Thinking Questions

These activities are designed to help you examine the material in this lesson in greater depth.

1. How does the 1912 sinking of the cruise ship *Titanic* illustrate the relationship between social stratification and life chances?

2. In the video "Ups and Downs" (Episode 9) we observe the success of Albanian immigrant Gloria Hamzai, who is able to own and operate her own business. Do you think Gloria's case is typical of most immigrants to the United States? Why or why not?

3. Do you think that poverty is primarily due to the way that society is organized, or a result of personal characteristics of persons who are poor? Explain.

TEST YOUR LEARNING

After answering the following questions, check your responses against the answer key at the end of this book. Review any questions that you answered incorrectly.

Multiple Choice

1. Sociologists assume that social stratification
   a. is a trait of society itself.
   b. reflects individual differences among people.
   c. does not exist in the United States.
   d. is the natural order of things.

2. A change in one's position in the social hierarchy, upward or downward, is referred to as
   a. social stratification.
   b. social mobility.
   c. the American Dream.
   d. the caste system.

3. Which of the following nations has a closed system of stratification?
   a. United States
   b. Great Britain
   c. Japan
   d. India

4. Dr. James is a college professor who enjoys the respect of the community but receives relatively low pay. His situation is an example of
   a. social mobility.
   b. Meritocracy.
   c. the Davis-Moore thesis.
   d. status inconsistency.

5. Who coined the term "survival of the fittest"?
   a. Charles Darwin
   b. Herbert Spencer
   c. Auguste Comte
   d. Karl Marx

6. The Davis-Moore thesis suggests that
   a. most people are poor because they are lazy.
   b. stratification benefits society as a whole.
   c. inequality tends to decline in industrial societies.
   d. class conflict will eventually result in revolution.

7. Social-conflict theories of stratification argue that
   a. stratification benefits society as a whole.
   b. stratification benefits certain people but not others.
   c. stratification will cease to exist in the twenty-first century.
   d. stratification is the result of individual differences among people.

8. After the U.S. Civil War, many Black former slaves worked the land under a system in which they borrowed from their landlord for equipment and seed to plant a crop and later paid the landlord out of the proceeds of the harvest. This system was known as
   a. piecework.
   b. sharecropping.
   c. redlining.
   d. crop rent.

9. How many social classes are there in the United States, according to sociologists?
   a. Two
   b. Three
   c. Seven
   d. Sociologists disagree about the number of social classes

10. Many "new rich" engage in _____, using expensive homes, automobiles, and other property as status symbols.
    a. social stratification
    b. social mobility
    c. status consistency
    d. conspicuous consumption

11. Dropping out of school, losing a job, and getting divorced are examples of
    a. upward social mobility.
    b. downward social mobility.
    c. relative poverty.
    d. absolute poverty.

12. According to the video "Ups and Downs" (Episode 9), the Fair Housing Act of 1935 explicitly mentioned _____ as a criterion to be used in considering loan applications.
    a. gender
    b. ethnicity
    c. religious affiliation
    d. race

Short Answer

13. How has discrimination in housing affected the economic situation of African-American families?

14. The "American Dream" assumes that upward social mobility is possible for all Americans. Is this an accurate assumption? Why or why not?

15. What role does ideology play in supporting existing systems of inequality?

Worlds Apart

OVERVIEW

After World War II, scholars classified nations according to the *three-worlds model*. Rich industrial nations were referred to as the *First World*. Less industrialized socialist countries such as the former Soviet Union were known as the *Second World,* and *Third World* nations were the world's poorest. This model was criticized for being inaccurate and biased, and it was replaced with a classification of nations into high-income, middle-income, and low-income categories. The economic and social inequality from one nation to another is referred to as *global stratification.*

The economy of high-income nations is based on advanced technology, factories, large machines, and capital. High-income nations contain about 18 percent of the world's people, but they receive 79 percent of global income. Middle-income countries are less technologically developed and less economically productive than high-income nations, and they are more densely populated. Countries classified as low-income generally have agrarian rather than industry-based economies. Hunger, disease, unsafe housing, and extreme poverty are the reality for many people in these nations. Other problems in these nations can include illiteracy, warfare, and slavery.

Sociologists identify two types of poverty. *Relative poverty* occurs when some people have fewer economic resources than others. *Absolute poverty*, on the other hand, refers to a lack of economic resources that is so severe it threatens life itself. The global extent of absolute poverty is shown by variations in the median age at death of a nation's population. Most deaths in rich nations occur among the elderly. In the world's poorest nations, about half of all deaths occur among children under age ten. Organizations such as the International Red Cross and Doctors Without Borders work to combat the effects of hunger among the world's poorest people.

About 15 million people die each year from causes relating to hunger. Most of them live in low-income countries. As shown in the video "Worlds Apart" (Episode 10), visitors to the poorest regions of the world are often shocked at the prevalence of malnutrition and disease. World poverty disproportionately affects women and children.

Scholars have identified a number of factors related to poverty around the world. Poor societies primarily use human and animal labor rather than more advanced technology. In addition, cultural patterns and traditions serve to make innovation difficult. Where wealth does exist in poor nations, it is unequally distributed. Furthermore, in low-income societies women are deprived of educational and employment opportunities, and they are expected to bear many children. Rich nations have contributed to keeping poor nations in an economically disadvantaged position through colonialism, neocolonialism, and the growing influence of multinational corporations.

Two major theoretical perspectives have been proposed to explain global inequality. *Modernization theory* suggests that the world's richest nations have been able to increase their levels of affluence due to advanced industrial technology. W. W. Rostow proposes that nations pass through four stages as industrial technology diffuses across the world. Nations in the traditional stage are poorest, with cultures based on traditional ways. Greater economic growth occurs in the take-off stage, due in large part to economic and technological assistance from richer nations. In the drive-to-technological-maturity stage, industrial technology becomes firmly established and traditional ways loosen their hold on the nation's people. Finally, economic development and levels of affluence reach their peak in the stage of high mass consumption.

Dependency theory explains global economic inequality as a result of the exploitation of poorer nations by richer ones. According to this theory, the foundation for dependency was laid late in the fifteenth century as more powerful nations began to make colonies out of poorer nations. Although formal colonialism no longer exists, dependency theorists argue that rich nations continue to dominate and exploit poor nations for economic gain. Immanuel Wallerstein expands on dependency theory by classifying nations into rich core nations, semi-peripheral nations, and poor peripheral nations. Both modernization theory and dependency theory have been criticized for being incomplete explanations, but taken together they provide a way of explaining global economic inequality and its attendant problems such as poverty and world hunger.

FOCUS YOUR ATTENTION

Assignments

Read the pages indicated for the text assigned by your instructor.

— *Sociology*, 10th Edition, by Macionis. Chapter 12, "Global Stratification," pages 298–323.

— *Society: The Basics,* 8th Edition, by Macionis. Chapter 9, "Global Stratification," pages 225–249.

Watch Episode 10, "Worlds Apart," after scanning the Video Focus Points.

Learning Objectives

After completing your study of this lesson, you should be familiar with the facts and concepts presented and should be able to:

1. Explain the extent of economic inequality among the nations of the world.

2. Differentiate among conditions in high-income, middle-income, and low-income countries.

3. Describe the extent of world poverty, and how it affects women and children.

4. Compare and contrast the explanations of global wealth and power suggested by dependency theory and modernization theory.

5. Describe the trends in global stratification in recent decades.

Key Terms and Concepts

The following terms are important to your understanding of the material presented in this lesson.

absolute poverty
chattel slavery
colonialism
core nations
debt bondage
dependency theory
first-world nations
globalization
gross domestic product
modernization theory
multinational corporation
neocolonialism
peripheral nations
relative poverty
second-world nations
semiperipheral nations
third-world nations
three-worlds model

Video Focus Points

The following points are designed to help you get the most out of the video for this lesson. Read them carefully before viewing the episode.

— There is a large gap between the richest and poorest Americans. However, the greatest economic inequality exists between the world's high-income nations and low-income nations.

— Many of the world's people live in absolute poverty, unable to afford the basic necessities of life.

— Poverty levels are especially high in the Southern Hemisphere, particularly on the continent of Africa.

— A nation's poverty level is related to its level of technological development.

— The increasing globalization of the world's economies benefits some people but negatively affects many others.

Text Focus Points

These are the main points presented in the text assignment for this lesson. Read them carefully before reading the text.

— Economic inequality is widespread across the nations of the world, with the richest nations receiving a large share of the world's income and the poorest nations receiving only a small amount.

— In the poorest nations of the world, millions of people live in absolute poverty.

— Global poverty disproportionately affects women and children.

— Factors that are related to a nation's level of poverty include technology, population growth, cultural patterns, social stratification, gender inequality, and global power relationships.

— Modernization theory suggests that improvements in industrial technology allow nations to raise their level of prosperity. Dependency theory sees the causes of economic inequality as the result of a pattern of exploitation of poor nations by richer nations.

Critical Thinking Questions

These activities are designed to help you examine the material in this lesson in greater depth.

1. According to sociologist Arlie Hochschild in the video "Worlds Apart" (Episode 10), richer nations are getting richer and poor nations are getting poorer. What can be done to halt this apparent trend?

2. Why does global poverty disproportionately affect women and children?

3. Why does global economic inequality exist, according to modernization theory and dependency theory? Which theory do you support and why? Use examples to support your argument, either from this lesson or from newspaper or journal articles you have found on the Internet.

TEST YOUR LEARNING

After answering the following questions, check your responses against the answer key at the end of this book. Review any questions that you answered incorrectly.

Multiple Choice

1. According to the United Nations Secretary-General, the wealth of the world's three richest *individuals* is approximately equal to the economic output of the world's _____ poorest *countries*.
   a. 8
   b. 18
   c. 28
   d. 48

2. One of the criticisms that has been leveled at the three-worlds model of global stratification is that changes in Eastern Europe, including the fall of the Soviet Union, mean that there is no longer a distinctive
   a. First World.
   b. Second World.
   c. Third World.
   d. Fourth World.

3. Models that classify the world's 192 nations into economic categories underestimate the extent of global inequality because
   a. they ignore inequality *within* nations.
   b. they fail to take *income levels* into account.
   c. they do not include *all* of the world's nations.
   d. they fail to take *inflation* into account.

4. Which of the following is classified as a *high-income country*?
   a. Ecuador
   b. Indonesia
   c. Ethiopia
   d. Argentina

5. Economic productivity is lowest in regions of the world where
   a. population growth is highest.
   b. population growth is stagnant.
   c. population growth is lowest.
   d. population growth is not measured.

6. The Gross Domestic Products (GDP) of the world's richest nations are _____ of times more productive than the poorest countries.
   a. hundreds
   b. thousands
   c. hundreds of thousands
   d. millions

7. One-third or more of the people who live in low-income countries experience _____, which means that they cannot afford the basic necessities of life.
   a. relative poverty
   b. subjective poverty
   c. absolute poverty
   d. transient poverty

8. Where are most of the world's poorest countries located?
   a. Northern Europe
   b. Western Hemisphere
   c. Northern Hemisphere
   d. Southern Hemisphere

9. In low-income countries, _____ of all deaths occur among children under the age of 10 years.
   a. one-eighth
   b. one-quarter
   c. one-half
   d. one-third

10. The type of slavery in which one person owns another is called
    a. chattel slavery.
    b. debt bondage.
    c. child slavery.
    d. servile marriage.

11. Which of the following terms refers to the worldwide process of cultural and economic integration?
    a. Multinationalism
    b. Multiculturalism
    c. Globalization
    d. Global inequality

12. According to the _____ model, rich nations such as the United States are economic role models for poor nations.
    a. three-worlds
    b. modernization
    c. stratification
    d. multicultural

Short Answer

13. Describe the reactions of physicians working for Doctors Without Borders as they observed levels of poverty at the border of Somalia, Ethiopia, and Kenya in 1996.

14. In what regions of the world is poverty most prevalent?

15. How widespread is slavery around the world? What are its various forms?

Venus and Mars

OVERVIEW

Sociologists use the term *sex* to refer to biological differences between males and females. *Gender*, on the other hand, is the personal traits and social positions that members of a society attach to being female or male. The social positioning that is a part of gender identification includes the hierarchical ranking of men and women. This unequal distribution of wealth, power, and privilege between men and women is known as *gender stratification*. Most sociologists believe that gender is primarily a product of social organization rather than biological necessity.

Every society in the world is organized to a greater or lesser extent as a *patriarchy*, which is a form of social organization in which males dominate females. There is considerable variation in women's social standing in relation to men's in societies around the world. And while matriarchal societies are theoretically possible, none have been known to exist. Women everywhere are subjected to *sexism*; the belief that one sex is innately superior to the other. Sexism exists at both individual and institutional levels.

Males and females are taught from an early age to behave according to society's expectations of appropriate male and female behavior. These *gender roles* are learned during the socialization process. The most important agents of socialization are the family, the school, the peer group, and the mass media. As illustrated by the female football team presented in the video "Venus and Mars"

(Episode 11) it can take a lot of determination to defy the agents of socialization in our society.

The inequality of gender stratification is clearly seen in the world of work, where traditional gender roles dictate that women should remain in the home and take care of child care and household tasks. In 1900, only about 20 percent of American women worked outside of the home. This situation changed greatly during the twentieth century, due in part to the growth and success of the feminist movement in the 60s and 70s, which helped to change the way people viewed the role of women in society. At the present time about 60 percent of adult women in the United States are in the labor force on a full-time or part-time basis. However, women tend to hold less prestigious jobs than men, and women earn less money than men do for performing the same work.

Even jobs themselves are gender stratified within American society. Certain jobs—like nursing—are primarily practiced by women, while jobs like construction remain the domain of men. According to sociologist Arlie Hochschild, the gender stratification continues at home. Most women who work outside the home, return to perform a "second shift" of housework and child care tasks. Gender stratification is found in other social institutions as well, including education, politics, and the military.

Some sociologists view women as a *minority group*, which is any category of people distinguished by physical or cultural differences that a society sets apart and subordinates. *Intersection theory* suggests that race, class, and gender combine to produce increased levels of economic and social disadvantage.

An important dimension of gender stratification in societies concerns the prevalence of violence against women. This violence can take many forms including physical violence, sexual harassment, and genital mutilation. Critics also view pornography as demeaning to women, thus further exacerbating the subordination of women. Others tolerate pornography as an expression of the right to free speech.

Structural-functional analysis suggests that traditional gender roles are beneficial to society as a whole. Social-conflict analysis focuses on the differing levels of power held by men and women, and the resulting domination of women in a patriarchal society. Those with a feminist perspective advocate social change to eliminate gender stratification completely.

FOCUS YOUR ATTENTION

Assignments

Read the pages indicated for the text assigned by your instructor.

— *Sociology*, 10th edition, by Macionis. Chapter 13, "Gender Stratification," pages 324–351.

— *Society: The Basics*, 8th edition, by Macionis. Chapter 10, "Gender Stratification," pages 250–277.

Watch Episode 11, "Venus and Mars," after scanning the Video Focus Points.

Learning Objectives

After completing your study of this lesson, you should be familiar with the facts and concepts presented and should be able to:

1. Explain the biological and social bases of gender inequality.

2. Understand how the socialization process shapes gender roles.

3. Explain the dimensions of gender stratification in society.

4. Understand the structural-functional, social-conflict, intersection theory, and feminist explanations of the social organization of gender.

Key Terms and Concepts

The following terms are important to your understanding of the material presented in this lesson.

feminism
gender
gender roles
gender stratification
intersection theory
matriarchy
minority
patriarchy
sexism
sexual harassment

Term undefined in the text:

second shift – Household and child care tasks performed by women who are employed outside of the home.

Video Focus Points

The following points are designed to help you get the most out of the video for this lesson. Read them carefully before viewing the episode.

— More and more women are becoming involved in traditionally male dominated activities such as football, and occupations such as firefighter.

— Gender roles are learned in early life through the socialization process.

— More women are entering the labor force, but studies suggest that women still perform most of the household tasks.

— Despite the gains achieved by the feminist movement, many women continue to face gender-based discrimination and lack of opportunity in the workplace.

Text Focus Points

These are the main points presented in the text assignment for this lesson. Read them carefully before reading the text.

— Males and females are biologically different, but the gender roles they play are determined by society, not biology.

— Major agents of gender role socialization include the family, the peer group, schools, and the mass media.

— Gender stratification is clearly seen in the world of work, where the position of women is subordinate to that of men.

— Gender stratification is found in other social institutions, including the family, education, politics, and the military.

— One illustration of gender stratification's existence throughout the world is the prevalence of violence against women in its various forms, from physical violence to sexual harassment to genital mutilation.

— Structural-functional theory views traditional gender roles as helpful to society. Social-conflict theory suggests that gender roles reflect power relationships found in the larger society. Feminism advocates gender equality and opposes patriarchal social organization.

Critical Thinking Questions

These activities are designed to help you examine the material in this lesson in greater depth.

1. To what extent are the behaviors of men and women determined by biology and by culture?

2. Gender roles are learned through socialization in the family, schools, peer groups, and other social groups. Why do you think the gender-related messages of these agents of socialization are so similar to each other?

3. What do you think are some positive and negative effects, for society as a whole, of women serving in the military?

TEST YOUR LEARNING

After answering the following questions, check your responses against the answer key at the end of this book. Review any questions that you answered incorrectly.

Multiple Choice

1. _____ refers to the personal traits and social positions that members of a society attach to being female or male.
   a. Sex
   b. Biology
   c. Gender
   d. Inequality

2. Most sociologists believe that gender roles are a product of
   a. biological differences between men and women.
   b. the natural way that men and women should act.
   c. inborn traits.
   d. cultural conventions.

3. Women who attended the Seneca Falls (NY) Convention in 1848 heard activist _____ call for expanded rights for women.
   a. Margaret Mead
   b. Margaret Higgins Sanger
   c. Simone De Beauvoir
   d. Elizabeth Cady Stanton

4. In general, males outperform females in what ways?
   a. Intelligence
   b. Leadership skills
   c. Upper body strength
   d. Longevity

5. Approximately what percentage of the world's societies contains some degree of patriarchy?
   a. 100 percent
   b. 80 percent
   c. 60 percent
   d. 40 percent

6. The belief that one sex is innately superior to the other is known as
   a. sexual harassment.
   b. sexism.
   c. stratification.
   d. discrimination.

7. Women who play on tackle-football teams are
   a. acting like women should act.
   b. defying traditional gender roles.
   c. conforming to traditional gender roles.
   d. victims of sexual harassment.

8. Research shows that
   a. it is not possible for a society to be organized as a matriarchy.
   b. men and women do not develop exclusively masculine or feminine personalities.
   c. personalities are determined at birth by the sex of the child.
   d. men live longer than women in every society across the world.

9. In 1900, 20 percent of women in the United States worked outside the home. What percent of U.S. women aged 16 and over worked outside the home in 2001/2002?
   a. 20 percent
   b. 40 percent
   c. 60 percent
   d. 80 percent

10. In the United States, working women tend to be concentrated in _____ jobs.
    a. white-collar
    b. blue-collar
    c. pink-collar
    d. green-collar

11. The feminist movement was originally mobilized by
    a. white, middle-class women.
    b. white, middle-class men.
    c. working-class minority women.
    d. working-class white women.

12. Critics of women in the military often point to which of the following factors to support their view?
    a. Women in the military are less educated than their male counterparts.
    b. Women in the military are less intelligent than their male counterparts.
    c. Most women are not as physically strong as most men.
    d. Most women are not mentally able to perform combat-related tasks.

Short Answer

13. What have been some of the results of the women's movement on gender inequality in the United States?

14. Explain the meaning of sociologist Arlie Hochschild's term "second shift."

15. What are the five basic ideas or general principles of feminism?

Colors

OVERVIEW

As you know from earlier lessons, social stratification is a system by which a society ranks categories of people in a hierarchy. Two of the characteristics used to rank people in society are race and ethnicity. Members of *racial groups* are identified by their shared biological characteristics, like skin color, while *ethnic group* members are identified by a common cultural heritage.

Race and ethnicity are socially constructed categories. Racial categories exist because society considers some physical traits to be important. Just as racial categories highlight physical traits as key sources of difference, ethnic categories focus on certain cultural aspects such as a common ancestry, language, or religion as the defining factors of a group's identity. Race and ethnicity are often related since members of some racial groups, such as Japanese Americans, may also share a common ethnic culture.

Racial and ethnic groups are often viewed as minorities in a population. A *minority* is defined in sociology as any category of people distinguished by physical or cultural differences that a society sets apart and subordinates. Minorities share a distinct identity and they are subject to subordination at the hands of the dominant group. In addition, racial and ethnic group membership often serves as a master status, or the characteristic that is viewed by society as a person's most important attribute over all others. While minorities are usually a small proportion of a society's population, in some cases they may actually have more members than the dominant group.

Racial and ethnic minorities are often subjected to prejudice, stereotyping, and discrimination at the hands of the dominant group. *Prejudice*—rigid and irrational generalizations about an entire category of people—is often based on *stereotypes*, which are exaggerated descriptions applied to every person in a particular category. An especially powerful and destructive form of prejudice is *racism*, which is the belief that one racial category is innately superior or inferior to another. For several hundred years, racism was the law of the land in the United States, as ideas about racial inferiority supported the enslavement of persons of African descent. Social scientists have proposed various theories that attempt to explain the origins of prejudice based on frustration (scapegoat theory), personality (authoritarian personality theory), culture (culture theory), and conflict (conflict theory).

While prejudice is a negative attitude, *discrimination* refers to actions that treat various categories of people unequally. Prejudice and discrimination often occur together, but non-prejudiced persons may also engage in discrimination through their actions. Individual persons may engage in prejudice and discrimination, but so can social institutions, such as the educational system. For instance, it wasn't until 1954 that the U.S. Supreme Court ruled in *Brown v. Board of Education* that discrimination in the nation's schools is unconstitutional. Prejudice and discrimination reinforce each other in a vicious circle, in which discriminatory actions against minority group members put them in a socially disadvantaged position that can be used as evidence to justify further prejudice and discrimination.

Majority groups and minority groups can interact with each other in several ways. Patterns of interaction include pluralism, assimilation, segregation, and genocide. In a *pluralistic* society, members of minority groups are distinct, but have equal social standing with all other members of the society. *Assimilation* occurs when minority group members adopt the cultural patterns of the dominant group in order to fit in with the larger society. *Segregation* is the physical and social separation of categories of people, like the segregation of whites and blacks that was practiced in the American South until the mid twentieth century. The most extreme treatment of minority groups is *genocide*, which is the systematic killing of one category of people by another, such as occurred during the Holocaust in World War II when the German Nazis inflicted genocide on people of Jewish descent.

Throughout the history of the United States, many racial and ethnic groups have been subject to varying degrees of prejudice and discrimination at the hands of the dominant group, the white Anglo-Saxon Protestants (WASPs). After the discovery of the New World, white Europeans engaged in a four hundred year program of discrimination and genocide directed at the Native Americans. Black Africans were forcibly captured and brought to North America, where they were sold as slaves. Their descendents, African Americans, while not enslaved, continue to experience prejudice and discrimination in our society. Asian and Hispanic Americans also continue to experience prejudice and discrimination, and despite their white skin, White ethnic Americans, like the Irish, Jews, and Italians have been mistreated at the hands of the dominant WASP majority at various points in our nation's history. More recently, in our post 9/11 society, Arab Americans and Muslims have been singled out as targets of racism and discrimination.

FOCUS YOUR ATTENTION

Assignments

Read the pages indicated for the text assigned by your instructor.

— *Sociology,* 10th Edition, by Macionis. Chapter 14, "Race and Ethnicity," pages 352–381.

— *Society, The Basics,* 8th Edition, by Macionis. Chapter 11, "Race and Ethnicity," pages 278–307.

Watch Episode 12, "Colors," after scanning the Video Focus Points.

Learning Objectives

After completing your study of this lesson, you should be familiar with the facts and concepts presented and should be able to:

1. Discuss the social meaning of race, ethnicity, and minority group status. Explain the importance of social constructions of race and ethnicity in the United States, both historically and in the present day.

2. Explain the nature of prejudice, including stereotypes and racism.

3. Understand four theories that have been proposed to explain the causes of prejudice.

4. Articulate the nature of discrimination at the individual level and the social institutional level, and how prejudice and discrimination combine to support and perpetuate each other.

5. Discuss the various patterns of interaction between majority groups and minority groups, including pluralism, assimilation, segregation, and genocide.

Key Terms

The following terms are important to your understanding of the material presented in this lesson. Terms appearing only in the video are defined.

assimilation
authoritarian personality theory (of prejudice)
discrimination

ethnicity
genocide
institutional prejudice and discrimination
master status
minority
pluralism
prejudice
race
racism
segregation
stereotyping
Thomas theorem
white ethnics
xenophobia

Terms undefined in the text:

bigotry – An attitude of narrow-minded intolerance toward others.

hate crime – A criminal act against a person or a person's property by an offender who is motivated by racial or other bias.

Video Focus Points

The following points are designed to help you get the most out of the video for this lesson. Read them carefully before viewing the episode.

— Members of ethnic groups, such as Arab Americans, often find that members of the dominant culture do not clearly understand their unique cultural attitudes and behaviors. Prejudice and discrimination are common. Throughout American history, minorities have been the victims of racial and ethnic prejudice, stereotyping, racism, discrimination, and even genocide.

— Sociologists point out that discrimination is usually based on stereotyping. For example, Muslims have been stereotyped and discriminated against since the terrorist attacks of September 11, 2001.

— Changes in the U.S. economy have disproportionately affected minority group members, as illustrated by the plight of disadvantaged African Americans living in decaying urban neighborhoods.

— The challenge for minority groups is to find ways to maintain their unique cultural identities in the midst of pressures to conform to mainstream culture.

— The new Arab-American Museum in Dearborn, Michigan may help to educate the non-Arabic public about Arab Americans and reduce the bigotry and stereotyping directed at this one particular ethnic group.

Text Focus Points

These are the main points presented in the text assignment for this lesson. Read them carefully before reading the text.

— Race and ethnicity are socially constructed categories; not biologically based. They are important because people define others in terms of their color (race) and their culture (ethnicity).

— Members of racial and ethnic minority groups are often victims of prejudice (biased attitudes) and discrimination (unequal treatment).

— Racism is a form of prejudice. It is the belief that one racial category is innately superior or inferior to another.

— Patterns of interaction between majority and minority group members include pluralism, assimilation, segregation, and genocide.

— In North America, African Americans and Native Americans have been subjected to extremely harsh treatment at the hands of white European settlers and their descendants. Most immigrants to the U.S. now come from Latin America and Asia rather than Europe.

Critical Thinking Questions

These activities are designed to help you examine the material in this lesson in greater depth.

1. Discuss the pros and cons of Affirmative Action. Do you think that Affirmative Action programs should continue? Why or why not?

2. Explain how prejudice and discrimination can perpetuate themselves in a society. Give specific examples.

3. Do you believe that America is a pluralistic society? Why or why not? Do you favor pluralism or assimilation of immigrants? Support your position.

TEST YOUR LEARNING

After answering the following questions, check your responses against the answer key at the end of this book. Review any questions that you answered incorrectly.

Multiple Choice

1. _____ refers to a socially constructed category composed of people who share biologically transmitted traits that members of a society consider important.
   a. Race
   b. Ethnicity
   c. Prejudice
   d. Assimilation

2. Nineteenth century biologists divided humans into three racial types. Which of the following is NOT one of these racial types?
   a. Caucasoid
   b. Negroid
   c. Asiatic
   d. Mongoloid

3. _____ refers to attitudes, while _____ refers to actions or behavior.
   a. Prejudice, stereotyping
   b. Stereotyping, prejudice
   c. Prejudice, discrimination
   d. Discrimination, prejudice

4. Catholics, Jews, Polish Americans, and Native Americans are examples of
   a. races.
   b. ethnic groups.
   c. stereotypes.
   d. scapegoats.

5. Research has shown that banks more frequently reject home mortgage applications from minorities, or give minority applicants less favorable terms than white applicants,

even when individuals have the same income and live in similar neighborhoods. This is an example of
   a. institutional pluralism and genocide.
   b. institutional xenophobia.
   c. institutional prejudice and discrimination.
   d. institutional assimilation.

6. Black South Africans are considered a minority in their country because
   a. they were brought to South Africa from eastern Africa by white settlers.
   b. they are racially different.
   c. they are only a small percentage of the South African population.
   d. they are culturally different.

7. A Russian immigrant family who speaks English with their children at home, sends their kids to local public schools, lives in a predominately white Anglo-Saxon neighborhood, but goes to a Russian bakery for bread, would most likely be an example of what type of interaction?
   a. Assimilation
   b. Pluralism
   c. Segregation
   d. Xenophobia

8. Arab Americans have sometimes been viewed as terrorists since the attacks on the United States on September 11, 2001. This is an example of
   a. discrimination.
   b. racism.
   c. symbolic interactionism.
   d. stereotyping.

9. The typical African American family has about _____ the assets or net worth of the typical white family.
   a. one-eighth
   b. one quarter
   c. one third
   d. one half

10. Which of the following theories of prejudice suggests that prejudice is caused by frustration among people who are themselves disadvantaged?
   a. Conflict theory
   b. Culture theory
   c. Authoritarian personality theory
   d. Scapegoat theory

11. Which of the following theories of prejudice suggests that powerful people use prejudice to justify oppressing others?
    a. Conflict theory
    b. Culture theory
    c. Authoritarian personality theory
    d. Scapegoat theory

12. Native Americans have been the victims of
    a. segregation.
    b. forced assimilation.
    c. genocide.
    d. all of the above.

Short Answer

13. Discuss some of the examples of prejudice toward minority group members in the United States.

14. Explain what sociologists mean when they say that race and ethnicity are social constructions.

15. Discuss the four patterns of interaction that may occur when minority groups come in contact with members of the majority group. Give examples of each.

Golden Years

OVERVIEW

During the twentieth century the population of Americans over the age of 65 increased by ten times and is expected to double again by 2030, when over half the nation's population will be over the age of 40. Two major factors have contributed to the increase in older people in the United States: a declining birth rate and an increase in life expectancy. The rapid increase in the life expectancy of Americans is referred to in the video "Golden Years" (Episode 13) as the *Longevity Revolution*. Other industrialized nations have experienced similar trends.

As people grow older they often must deal with a host of physical and psychological changes. There are two groups of elderly: the "young old," typically seen as those between the ages of 65 and 75, and the "old old," those people age 75 and above. Health issues become more important in later stages of the life cycle, and society must adapt by providing medical care and other services. Treatment of the elderly varies from one society to another. In preindustrial societies, older persons are often treated with great respect. As societies industrialize, the elderly are increasingly viewed as marginal to society.

The elderly must find meaning in their lives, apart from the social roles they have left behind after retiring from the workplace. Social isolation is common, especially for women who have outlived their husbands. Although today's elder population is generally financially better off than the elderly 30 to 50 years ago, many older persons live in poverty and have difficulty obtaining care that will allow them to maintain an adequate quality of life. Usually the elderly who live in poverty are women, members of minority groups, and those who would be identified as the "old old." Most elder care is provided by family members, although some older persons are cared for in nursing homes or assisted living centers. The elderly often become victims of age stratification, ageism, elder abuse, and stereotyping, to the extent that some analysts treat the elderly as a minority group.

Disengagement theory suggests that society disengages older people from social roles so that social organization remains orderly and efficient. Activity theory, a variant of symbolic-interaction analysis, suggests that older persons need to find new roles to replace the ones they have left behind. Social-conflict analysis points to the power differences between older persons and younger persons, which are often related to variations in the availability of monetary resources.

Death and dying are issues of particular concern to society's oldest members. Death is separated from everyday existence in the United States, which makes it more difficult to deal with. The death of a spouse is a very upsetting event, and the "oldest old" must prepare for their own deaths. The process of dying often brings up ethical issues such as the right to die, living wills, and euthanasia.

During the twenty-first century, the United States and other high-income nations must work to solve many pressing issues relating to the increased number of elderly citizens. These issues include medical care, finances, caregiving, and the social roles that the elderly will play in the society of the future.

FOCUS YOUR ATTENTION

Assignments

Read the pages indicated for the text assigned by your instructor.

— *Sociology,* 10th Edition, by Macionis. Chapter 15, "Aging and the Elderly," pages 382–405. Review Chapter 5, "Socialization," pages 124–125.

— *Society, The Basics,* 8th Edition, by Macionis. Chapter 11, "Race and Ethnicity."
Chapter 3, "Socialization", pages 70 and 77–80
Chapter 8, "Social Stratification," page 216
Chapter 13, "Family and Religion," page 354
Chapter 14, "Education and Health," pages 397–399, 403–404
Chapter 15, "Population, Urbanization, and Environment," pages 419–425
Chapter 16, "Social Change: Modern and Postmodern Societies," page 453

Watch Episode 13, "Golden Years" after scanning the Video Focus Points.

Learning Objectives

After completing your study of this lesson, you should be familiar with the facts and concepts presented and should be able to:

1. Explain why the percentage of older persons is increasing in the United States and other industrialized nations of the world.

2. Understand how the way that older persons are viewed by society varies from one culture to another.

3. List and describe the biological and psychological changes that affect persons during later stages of the life cycle.

4. Explain how the elderly are cared for in the United States.

5. Understand how issues of illness and death affect society's oldest members.

Key Terms and Concepts

The following terms are important to your understanding of the material presented in this lesson.

age stratification
ageism
caregiving
euthanasia
gerontocracy
gerontology
life expectancy

Terms undefined in the text:

activity theory – The belief that a high level of activity increases personal satisfaction in old age.

disengagement theory – The idea that society enhances its orderly operation by removing people from positions of responsibility as they reach old age.

Longevity Revolution – The fact that life expectancy has nearly doubled since 1900 in the United States.

Video Focus Points

The following points are designed to help you get the most out of the video for this lesson. Read them carefully before viewing the episode.

— Nursing homes and assisted living facilities struggle to provide quality care with limited resources.

— The life expectancy of Americans has nearly doubled since 1900, a trend that is referred to as the Longevity Revolution.

— Longer life expectancy has resulted in a significant increase in the number of older persons in the United States.

— Older persons often face issues of health and illness, finances, and growing dependency on others.

Text Focus Points

These are the main points presented in the text assignment for this lesson. Read them carefully before reading the text.

— In the past 100 years life expectancy has doubled and the number of older Americans has greatly increased.

— Older persons face concerns relating to physical and mental health, finances, and dependency on others.

— Persons in their final years of life must deal with issues surrounding death and dying.

— Older persons are often stereotyped as dissatisfied, disabled, and unproductive.

— As the population of older Americans increases, plans must be made to provide quality care for the elderly during their later years.

Critical Thinking Questions

These activities are designed to help you examine the material in this lesson in greater depth.

1. Do you think it should be legal for physicians to actively assist in the deaths of terminally-ill patients who wish to die? Why or why not?

2. What cultural factors make the situation of the "sandwich generation" (Baby Boomers) especially difficulty in regard to the care of elderly parents?

3. What emotional issues are often faced by elderly persons living in nursing homes or assisted-living homes? Do you think such concerns are justified? Why or why not?

TEST YOUR LEARNING

After answering the following questions, check your responses against the answer key at the end of this book. Review any questions that you answered incorrectly.

Multiple Choice

1. According to Erik Erikson, the primary challenge of old age is
   a. integrity versus despair.
   b. making a difference versus self-absorption.
   c. gaining identity versus confusion.
   d. industriousness versus inferiority.

2. The study of aging and the elderly is known as
   a. epidemiology.
   b. gerontology.
   c. gerontocracy.
   d. thanatology.

3. Which of the following types of society is most likely to be a gerontocracy?
   a. Preindustrial
   b. Industrial
   c. Information-oriented
   d. Postindustrial

4. Which of the following is NOT one of Elizabeth Kubler-Ross's five stages of reaction to dying?
   a. Denial
   b. Anger
   c. Resonance
   d. Negotiation

5. In 2001, the poverty rate for United States residents over age 65 was
   a. well below the national average.
   b. slightly below the national average.
   c. slightly above the national average.
   d. well above the national average.

6. Due to increased life expectancy, the population of the United States is
   a. becoming less prosperous.
   b. growing older.
   c. growing more prosperous.
   d. becoming younger.

7. The increased life span of Americans during the past 100 years is referred to in the video "Golden Years" (Episode 13) as
   a. the life-span revolution.
   b. the golden age.
   c. the gilded revolution.
   d. the Longevity Revolution.

8. In the United States, women generally outlive men because
   a. men have a longer life expectancy than women.
   b. women have a longer life expectancy than men.
   c. women tend to marry men who are younger than themselves.
   d. health care tends to be better for women than for men.

9. According to the U.S. Census Bureau, which of the following groups had the highest rate of poverty in 2001?
   a. Persons under age 18
   b. Persons age 25–34
   c. Persons age 55–59
   d. Persons age 65 and older

10. The "Right to Die" issue concerns
   a. whether terminally ill patients should be legally able to commit suicide.
   b. whether the courts should be allowed to terminate the life of terminally ill persons.
   c. whether physicians should be allowed to refuse to treat AIDS patients.
   d. whether physicians should be allowed to assist persons in ending their lives.

11. According to the video "Golden Years" (Episode 13), most people in Glen Elder, Jr.'s survey of people in the Midwest said that old age begins at age
   a. 55.
   b. 65.
   c. 75.
   d. 85.

12. Statistically, death is _____ among young people in the United States.
   a. rare
   b. somewhat common
   c. extremely common
   d. No data are available on this issue.

Short Answer

13. How do the cultures of Eastern and Western nations differ in respect to views of the elderly?

14. What changes have taken place in American society as a result of the large increase in the over-65 population since 1900?

15. What are some ethical issues surrounding death in the United States?

Working World

OVERVIEW

Social institutions such as the family, education, religion, law, the economy, and government are created to meet the fundamental needs of a society. The *economy* is perhaps the most important of these because it organizes the production, distribution, and consumption of goods and services. In this way the economy influences the entire society.

Throughout human history, societies have exhibited different economic structures that have been closely tied to the society's means of subsistence. In hunting and gathering societies, there is no organized economy because goods and services are allocated by the family.

The Agricultural Revolution made it possible for societies to create a surplus of food and other goods. Work became specialized as people concentrated on particular tasks such as raising animals or building dwellings.

The invention of the steam engine in 1765 made work much more efficient than relying on the muscle power of animals or humans. The resulting Industrial Revolution led to the centralization of work in factories. This fundamentally changed the nature of work, as people left rural areas to find work in the factory towns. Industrial work was impersonal, mechanized, and highly specialized. Employees worked for wages, often under very harsh conditions. Women and children were subjected to exploitation.

The Information Revolution of the *postindustrial economy* arose after World War II with the advent of highly automated machinery and the computer. The percentage of workers in the United States who are members of *labor unions* has declined as manufacturing jobs have shifted overseas. Most workers are now part of the service sector rather than the manufacturing or agricultural sectors. Work has shifted from tangible products to ideas, from mechanical skills to literacy skills, and from factory-based locations to widespread and decentralized locations.

In the United States, only about two percent of workers are engaged in the *primary sector* of the economy—that part of the economy that draws raw materials from the natural environment. More workers are involved in *secondary sector* production of manufactured goods from raw materials. However, the majority of workers in the U.S. and other high-income nations are employed in *tertiary sector* jobs, which involve the provision of services rather than the production of goods.

Since the end of World War II in 1945, the economies of the world's nations have become increasingly globalized. *Capitalism* has emerged as a more productive system than *socialism*. In the video "Working World," the situation faced by striking grocery store workers illustrates some of the frustrations experienced by employees in today's changing global economy. The video also shows the many ways that corporations must change the way they do business in order to adapt. Goods and services are now produced by multinational companies that operate across national borders. National governments have experienced difficulty regulating this new type of international economic structure. Some observers suggest that the United Nations will rise as a type of world government in order to regulate the new *global economy* of the twenty-first century.

FOCUS YOUR ATTENTION

Assignments

Read the pages indicated for the text assigned by your instructor.

— *Sociology*, 10th edition, by Macionis. Chapter 16, "The Economy and Work," pages 406–431.

— *Society: The Basics*, 8th edition, by Macionis. Chapter 12, "The Economy and Politics," pages 308–324 and 340–343.

Watch Episode 14, "Working World," after scanning the Video Focus Points.

Learning Objectives

After completing your study of this lesson, you should be familiar with the facts and concepts presented and should be able to:

1. Explain how the economic position of workers in the United States is affected by changes in the global economy.

2. Compare and contrast capitalist and socialist economic systems.

3. Discuss the tension in a capitalist system between the pursuit of corporate profits and the protection of workers' rights.

4. Understand how the nature of work changes under agricultural, industrial, and postindustrial economic systems.

5. Explain the role of the multinational corporation in today's global economy.

Key Terms and Concepts

The following terms are important to your understanding of the material presented in this lesson.

capitalism
communism
conglomerate
corporation
economy
global economy
labor union
monopoly
oligopoly
postindustrial economy
primary labor market
primary sector
profession
secondary labor market
secondary sector
social institution
socialism
state capitalism
tertiary sector
underground economy
welfare capitalism

Terms undefined in the text:

capital flight – Movement of corporate capital funds from one country to another for purposes of building facilities such as factories.

globalization – The process of change from nation-based economies to a global economy.

Video Focus Points

The following points are designed to help you get the most out of the video for this lesson. Read them carefully before viewing the episode.

— Economic globalization has resulted in many changes for American workers, including the loss of jobs to workers from other nations who will accept lower wages and fewer benefits. However, some analysts argue that companies must embrace globalization in order to compete in the world economy.

— Labor unions allow workers to put pressure on employers through collective action, but strikes and lockouts can be costly for owners and employees alike.

— In the United States, the change from manufacturing jobs to service jobs has resulted in a rise in the number of jobs with low pay and few or no benefits such as health insurance.

— As the world's economic structures become increasingly globalized, many people wonder who will control the expanding power of global conglomerates. Some scholars suggest that the United Nations will evolve into an instrument of world government. National cultures are strong, however, and national governments can be expected to resist this trend.

Text Focus Points

These are the main points presented in the text assignment for this lesson. Read them carefully before reading the text.

— The economy is perhaps the most influential social institution because it determines how goods and services are allocated in society. The economic structure of a society determines who gets what.

— Economies vary according to type of production, level of technology, focus on goods or services, and political organization. Economies range from agrarian to postindustrial, with capitalist or socialist political structures.

— Economic inequality affects groups of people within a society because some groups have more goods and services than others. Economic inequality exists between nations as well.

— Multinational corporations have become increasingly influential, affecting the lives of Americans as well as the lives of citizens of other nations.

— The twenty-first century will continue to see the expansion of the global economy, in which the economies of all of the world's nations are increasingly intertwined.

Critical Thinking

These activities are designed to help you examine the material in this lesson in greater depth.

1. Which system of economic and political organization would you define as "better," capitalism or socialism? Explain the criteria upon which you base your answer.

2. Discuss the role of labor unions in the United States workplace. What factors have led to the relative decline in union membership in the past half century?

3. Discuss some positive and negative consequences of the rise of the computer in the postindustrial economy.

TEST YOUR LEARNING

After answering the following questions, check your responses against the answer key at the end of this book. Review any questions that you answered incorrectly.

Multiple Choice

1. About 5000 years ago, humans experienced the Agricultural Revolution. The four factors that arose from the Agricultural Revolution and led to the creation of the economy as a distinct social institution were agricultural technology, job specialization, trade, and
   a. permanent settlements.
   b. development of coins and paper money.
   c. hunting and gathering.
   d. creation of factories.

2. The _____ is the part of the economy that transforms raw materials into manufactured goods.
   a. primary sector
   b. secondary sector
   c. tertiary sector
   d. postindustrial sector

3. Which of the following economic systems is the most economically productive?
   a. Capitalism
   b. Socialism
   c. Communism
   d. All of these economic systems are equally productive

4. Which of the following is NOT one of the major consequences of the development of a global economy?
   a. Different regions of the world specialize in different sectors of economic activity
   b. An increasing number of products pass through more than one nation
   c. National governments no longer control the economic activity within their own borders
   d. Economic inequality between nations is greatly reduced

5. The shrinking role of the primary sector in the U.S. economy is illustrated by the fact that in 1900, 40 percent of U.S. workers were farmers but in 2001, about _____ were in agriculture.
   a. 1 percent
   b. 12 percent
   c. 20 percent
   d. 32 percent

6. A *profession* is a prestigious, white-collar occupation that requires extensive formal education. Which of the following is NOT one of the characteristics of a profession?
   a. Theoretical knowledge
   b. Community orientation rather than self-interest
   c. Authority over clients
   d. Government control of education and training

7. During the latter half of the twentieth century the U.S. economy transformed itself from a _____ economy to a _____ economy.
   a. service, manufacturing
   b. manufacturing, service
   c. agricultural, manufacturing
   d. manufacturing, agricultural

8. Between 1900 and 2000, the racial and gender composition of the U.S. work force
   a. became more diverse.
   b. remained about the same.
   c. became less diverse.
   d. No data are available to answer this question

9. The number of American workers who are members of a labor union has _____ since 1970.
   a. increased
   b. remained about the same
   c. decreased
   d. No data are available to answer this question

10. A major technological innovation that helped give rise to the Industrial Revolution was
    a. the hoe.
    b. the airplane.
    c. the automobile.
    d. the steam engine.

11. The idea that government should not interfere in any way with corporate decision-making is termed
    a. monopoly.
    b. oligarchy.
    c. deregulation.
    d. globalization.

12. Some nations in Western Europe, including Sweden and Italy, have a market-based economy but also offer broad social welfare programs. This type of economic system is known as
    a. socialism.
    b. welfare capitalism.
    c. state capitalism.
    d. communism.

Short Answer

13. In what ways does the strike by the Southern California grocery workers, shown in the video "Working World," illustrate the global nature of economic issues?

14. Discuss the differences among agricultural, industrial, and postindustrial economies.

15. How has the nature of work changed for American employees during the past century?

Balance of Power

OVERVIEW

Power makes the world go 'round. And *politics* is the social institution that distributes the power, sets a society's agenda, and makes its decisions. The political business of a society and the exercise of its power are handled by its *government*. Power that is seen as legitimate by a society's people is referred to as *authority*. In order to gain the support of the people, governments strive to establish their power as legitimate in the eyes of the people, thus transforming it into authority. Sociologist Max Weber noted three types of authority employed by societies depending on their level of economic development: traditional, rational-legal, and charismatic authority.

The world's political systems conform to one of four types: monarchical, democratic, authoritarian, or totalitarian. *Monarchies* are ruled by hereditary nobles such as kings and queens. In constitutional monarchies, nobles act as symbolic figureheads while actual power is held by elected officials. In a *democracy*, the people exercise power either directly or by voting for elected officials. One type of direct participation by the American people in the democratic political process is ballot initiatives, such as California's Propositions 68 and 71, shown in the video "Balance of Power" (Episode 15). *Authoritarian* governments do not allow their people to have any voice at all in the political process. People's lives are most strictly regulated in *totalitarian* societies, which require total obedience to the government. Some analysts suggest that the world is moving toward a global political system

due to the effects of computers, instantaneous communication, and the influence of nongovernmental organizations (NGOs).

The United States was founded on the ideals of individualism and limited government. However, critics argue that the U.S. has become a *welfare state* because of the large number of government agencies and programs that provide benefits to the population.

The U.S. political spectrum includes conservative beliefs on the right and liberal beliefs on the left. Many citizens classify themselves as ideologically "middle of the road." Political parties are made up of people who occupy similar places on the political spectrum. The Republican Party is traditionally conservative while the Democratic Party traditionally espouses liberal ideas. Some people belong to other political parties, while some identify with no party at all. The U.S. political process depends on the participation of the citizenry, but many people who are eligible to vote do not do so because of indifference to or alienation from the process.

Three theoretical perspectives offer differing views of the nature of power in society. The *pluralist model* suggests that power is widely diffused among many competing interest groups that negotiate and compromise with each other in the political process. The *power-elite model* sees most political power residing among society's richest people and groups, especially leaders of the economy, government, and the military. The *Marxist*

63

model locates the source of political power in capitalism itself, which divides society into a mass of powerless people and a small group of people who are extremely wealthy and powerful.

Political controversies are usually resolved within existing legal and political structures. However, *political revolution* and *terrorism* involve efforts to achieve change by using means that are "beyond the rules." An extreme means of achieving political change is *warfare*, involving armed conflict between governments. Warfare and militarism have been common throughout human history. The presence of nuclear weapons, however, vastly increases the destructive potential of warfare. Given this increased destructive potential, an important goal of the 21st century is to prevent war and find nonviolent means of resolving political disputes.

FOCUS YOUR ATTENTION

Assignments

Read the pages indicated for the text assigned by your instructor.

— *Sociology*, 10th edition, by Macionis. Chapter 17, "Politics and Government," pages 432–458.

— *Society: The Basics*, 8th edition, by Macionis. Chapter 12, "Economics and Politics," pages 324–342.

Watch Episode 15, "Balance of Power," after scanning the Video Focus Points.

Learning Objectives

After completing your study of this lesson, you should be familiar with the facts and concepts presented and should be able to:

1. Identify the distinguishing features of the following types of political systems: monarchical, democratic, authoritarian, and totalitarian.

2. Describe politics in the United States, with emphasis on the political spectrum, political parties, voter participation, and special-interest groups.

3. Discuss the basic assumptions of the following theoretical analyses of politics: the pluralism model, the power-elite model, and the Marxist model.

4. Discuss the nature of political revolution and terrorism, and how these concepts are related.

5. Understand the nature of war and peace in a global context.

Key Terms and Concepts

The following terms are important to your understanding of the material presented in this lesson.

authoritarianism
authority
democracy
government
Marxist political-economy model
militarism
military-industrial complex
monarchy
pluralist model
political revolution
politics
power
power-elite model
routinization of charisma
terrorism
totalitarianism
war
welfare state

Video Focus Points

The following points are designed to help you get the most out of the video for this lesson. Read them carefully before viewing the episode.

— The nature of political participation can be seen in California's ballot initiatives such as Proposition 68, intended to expand legalized gambling and Proposition 71, supporting stem cell research.

— Levels of participation in the political process varies by sex, race, income, and education.

— Special interest groups lobby government officials in an attempt to affect change that is beneficial to their members.

— Political parties play an important role in the United States political process.

Text Focus Points

These are the main points presented in the text assignment for this lesson. Read them carefully before reading the text.

— Politics is the social institution that distributes power, sets a society's agenda, and makes decisions.

— Most of the world's political systems approximate one of the following types: monarchical, democratic, authoritarian, or totalitarian.

— Politics in the United States is based on individualism. Attitudes about certain political, economic, and social issues range from conservative to liberal, with most people identifying themselves as moderates. Voting in a democracy is a right, although in America most eligible voters do not exercise that right.

— Differing views of the role of power are suggested by the pluralist model, the power-elite model, and the Marxist model.

— Revolution and terrorism are means of achieving political ends by using methods that are beyond the rules.

— Nuclear weapons, militarism, and warfare are urgent problems that must be addressed for the good of all humanity.

Critical Thinking Questions

These activities are designed to help you examine the material in this lesson in greater depth.

1. The video "Balance of Power" (Episode 15) illustrates the controversial nature of gambling on Indian reservations. What does this issue suggest about the nature of power and politics in the United States?

2. Some analysts are critical of the power exerted over the political process by highly funded special-interest groups. Do you agree, or do you see special-interest groups as an effective way for people to have their voices heard in Washington?

3. Some have claimed that one man's terrorist is another man's freedom fighter or revolutionary. Do you agree with this statement?

TEST YOUR LEARNING

After answering the following questions, check your responses against the answer key at the end of this book. Review any questions that you answered incorrectly.

Multiple Choice

1. The political system in the kingdom of Saudi Arabia is a type of
   a. monarchy.
   b. democracy.
   c. authoritarianism.
   d. totalitarianism.

2. Industrialization and _____ tend to occur together because both require people who can read and write.
   a. monarchy
   b. democracy
   c. authoritarianism
   d. totalitarianism

3. What percent of Americans describe themselves as politically middle of the road?
   a. 17 percent
   b. 38 percent
   c. 57 percent
   d. 77 percent

4. The government of North Korea requires strict obedience and loyalty from all citizens. Which type of political system does this illustrate?
   a. Monarchy
   b. Democracy
   c. Authoritarianism
   d. Totalitarianism

5. Which of the following ideological positions is on the right side of the political spectrum?
   a. Democratic
   b. Liberal
   c. Middle of the road
   d. Conservative

6. Which of the following theoretical perspectives views power as widely dispersed across many competing interest groups?
   a. The power-elite model
   b. The Marxist model
   c. The pluralist model
   d. All of these theoretical perspectives view power as widely dispersed

7. In the United States, women have legally been able to vote since
   a. after the Revolutionary War.
   b. after the Civil War.
   c. after World War I.
   d. after World War II.

8. Which of the following terms best describes American political culture, as expressed in the Bill of Rights?
   a. Authoritarianism
   b. Partisanship
   c. Revolution
   d. Individualism

9. Members of which of the following groups tend to hold liberal views on economic issues?
   a. Higher-income people
   b. Members of the Republican Party
   c. African-Americans
   d. Members of the National Rifle Association

10. The National Rifle Association is an example of a
   a. government agency.
   b. special-interest group.
   c. PAC.
   d. political party.

11. Why does the American Association of Retired Persons (AARP) exert such a strong influence on American politics?
   a. It has an influential political action committee (PAC)
   b. It makes substantial "hard money" contributions to political candidates
   c. It contributes a large amount of "soft money"
   d. It has many members

12. The United States has been referred to as a _____ because of the many government-funded programs and agencies that provide benefits to the population.
   a. monarchy
   b. welfare state
   c. plutocracy
   d. totalitarian state

Short Answer

13. What role does money play in the United States political process?

14. What are the primary differences between the following types of political systems: monarchy, democracy, authoritarianism, and totalitarianism?

15. According to Quincy Wright, under what circumstances do humans go to war?

Family Matters

OVERVIEW

The *family* is a social institution that unites people in cooperative groups to oversee the bearing and raising of children. Family patterns vary within the United States and across other cultures of the world. The *nuclear family* is made up of one or two parents and their children; *extended families* include other kin as well. Sociologists also recognize the existence of *families of affinity*, which are made up of people with or without legal or blood ties who identify themselves as a family unit.

Families are usually based on a *marriage*, which is a legal relationship that is expected to be long-term, involving economic cooperation as well as sexual activity and childbearing. Marriage patterns exhibit global variations, but *monogamy* (marriage of two people) is most common. Some cultures allow *polygamy*, which is marriage to multiple spouses at one time.

Theoretical approaches offer guidelines for understanding the nature of the family. The structural-functional perspective emphasizes important functions that the institution of family performs for society as a whole. Families provide care and socialization of children, regulate sexual activity, clarify social identity, and offer emotional and economic security. The social-conflict approach is critical of the structural-functional view. It points out that the family perpetuates the same inequality patterns, such as patriarchy, that exist in the wider society. The symbolic-interaction approach focuses on individual experiences of family members. The social-exchange perspective suggests that court-ship and marriage involve negotiation as each partner attempts to maximize his or her advantages.

American cultural norms dictate that marriage be based on romantic love, but this is not true in all cultures. People may have marriage partners assigned by their families (arranged marriages), or they may marry for economic or other reasons. Research suggests that romantic love may provide a less stable foundation for marriage than other social or economic considerations because romantic love may fade over time. Married persons in all cultures must reconcile idealized views of marriage with their real experiences. In America, divorce is common. Approximately 90 percent of Americans marry at some point in their lives, but 40 percent of marriages end in divorce. On the other hand, most divorced persons remarry.

Family violence is not uncommon, and it often goes unreported. Marriage and family life are also influenced by inequalities of social class, ethnicity, race, and gender.

The traditional family form involves two parents of opposite sexes and their children. In recent decades a variety of alternative family forms have become more common. These include one-parent families, cohabiting couples, and gay and lesbian couples like those we meet in the video "Family Matters" (Episode 16). U.S. law has been slow to sanction alternative family forms, but an increasing number of U.S. states have adopted laws recognizing the legal rights of persons in non-traditional marriage and family relationships. It is clear that the postmodern family of the twenty-first century involves ever greater diversity of family types and more choices for family members.

FOCUS YOUR ATTENTION

Assignments

Read the pages indicated for the text assigned by your instructor.

— *Sociology*, 10th edition, by Macionis. Chapter 18, "Family," pages 460–487.

— *Society: The Basics*, 8th edition, by Macionis. Chapter 13, "Family and Religion," pages 344–363 and 376–378.

Watch Episode 16, "Family Matters," after scanning the Video Focus Points.

Learning Objectives

After completing your study of this lesson, you should be familiar with the facts and concepts presented and should be able to:

1. Explain the nature of the family as a social institution according to the structural-functional, social-conflict, and symbolic-interaction theoretical perspectives.

2. Illustrate variations in family types and marriage patterns in the United States and around the world.

3. Explain how family forms in the United States are related to social class, race/ethnicity, and gender.

4. Discuss the transitions and difficulties associated with family life in its various stages throughout the life course, including the problems of divorce and family violence.

5. Show how the American family has become increasingly diverse in recent decades.

Key Terms and Concepts

The following terms are important to your understanding of the material presented in this lesson.

cohabitation
descent
endogamy
exogamy
extended family
family
family of affinity
family unit
homogamy
incest taboo
kinship
marriage
monogamy
nuclear family
polygamy

Term undefined in the text:

civil union – A legally recognized agreement between two partners of the same sex, conferring some but not all of the rights of marriage.

Video Focus Points

The following points are designed to help you get the most out of the video for this lesson. Read them carefully before viewing the episode.

— The traditional definition of the American family has been expanded to include new forms such as same-sex couples with children.

— State governments in the United States have been very slow to allow civil unions and same-sex marriages. Legal challenges continue.

— Attitudes and behaviors surrounding marriage and family changed in the 1960s as oral contraceptives became readily available and as women entered the workforce in increased numbers. One of the biggest changes was the idea that marriage is not just a social institution created to raise children.

— Despite the changing attitudes and behaviors surrounding marriage, research shows that traditional gender roles still exert considerable power in the American family.

Text Focus Points

These are the main points presented in the text assignment for this lesson. Read them carefully before reading the text.

— The family is an important social institution, usually based on the marriage relationship, and often organized around the raising of children.

— Families serve many important functions: socialization of children, regulation of sexual activity, social placement, and material and emotional security.

— Families perpetuate patterns of patriarchal social inequality seen in the wider society.

— Ideal notions of marriage and the family must be reconciled with real-world issues throughout the various stages of family life. These issues include the problems of divorce, poverty, and family violence.

— Alternative family forms such as cohabitation, same-sex marriage, and one-parent families have become more common in recent decades.

Critical Thinking Questions

These activities are designed to help you examine the material in this lesson in greater depth.

1. Why do you think the idea of gay marriage is so controversial in American society?

2. In what ways does the family perpetuate social inequality, according to the social-conflict perspective? Provide specific examples.

3. Over the past century the United States divorce rate has exhibited a steady upward trend. Does this mean that marriage has become obsolete?

TEST YOUR LEARNING

After answering the following questions, check your responses against the answer key at the end of this book. Review any questions that you answered incorrectly.

Multiple Choice

1. Which of the following practices is LEAST common worldwide?
   a. Polygyny
   b. Patrilocality
   c. Polyandry
   d. Patrilineal descent

2. A family unit that includes parents and children as well as other kin is
   a. a nuclear family.
   b. an extended family.
   c. a tribe.
   d. a civil union.

3. The family is, in all instances,
   a. a social institution.
   b. a religious institution.
   c. related by blood ties.
   d. a marriage unit.

4. A New York City woman and her two children share an apartment with her female friend and her friend's male partner, and they all consider themselves to be a family. Which term best describes their family situation?
   a. Extended family
   b. Consanguine family
   c. Nuclear family
   d. Family of affinity

5. In societies with patrilineal descent, property is passed from
   a. mothers to daughters.
   b. fathers to sons.
   c. mothers to sons.
   d. fathers to daughters.

6. Which of the following theoretical perspectives suggests that the family perpetuates inequality by handing down property from one generation to the next?
   a. Structural-Functional Analysis
   b. Social-Conflict Analysis
   c. Symbolic-Interaction Analysis
   d. Social-Exchange Analysis

7. Which of the following statements is true about the post-modern family?
   a. There are many different types of family.
   b. The traditional family structure has become more common.
   c. Gay marriage is becoming less common.
   d. Gay couples do not adopt children.

8. Being a single mother increases a woman's risk of
   a. homogamy.
   b. poverty.
   c. polygamy.
   d. cohabitation.

9. Approximately what percentage of Americans marry at some point in their lives?
   a. 30 percent
   b. 50 percent
   c. 70 percent
   d. 90 percent

10. What percentage of divorced Americans re-marry?
    a. 20 percent
    b. 40 percent
    c. 60 percent
    d. 80 percent

11. Which of the following statements is true?
    a. Men do most of the housework in two-income families.
    b. Men do about half of the housework in two-income families.
    c. Women do two to three times as much housework as men.
    d. Women do all of the housework.

12. Why is the U.S. divorce rate so high?
    a. Americans value individualism.
    b. Romantic love often fades.
    c. Divorce is socially acceptable.
    d. The high divorce rate has many causes, not just one.

Short Answer

13. How have definitions of the American family changed since the 1960s?

14. How do marriage and kinship patterns vary around the world?

15. What social functions does the family perform according to the structural-functional approach?

LESSON 17

In God We Trust

OVERVIEW

One of the most important social institutions is *religion*. It is based on *faith*, which is belief that is founded on conviction rather than on direct experience or scientific evidence. Religion divides behavior and objects into two categories: sacred and profane. *Sacred* objects, events, and experiences are set apart as extraordinary, inspiring awe and reverence. They are often addressed with formal ceremonial behavior, or *rituals*. On the other hand, ordinary and everyday objects, events, and experiences are defined as *profane*. Sociology does not evaluate the correctness or accuracy of religious beliefs. Rather, sociologists study the ways that people act on their religious beliefs, and the forms that religious activity takes in various societies around the world.

Three main theoretical perspectives are used by sociologists to guide their thinking about religion. Emile Durkheim's structural-functional approach suggests that people are actually worshipping society itself through their religious beliefs and practices. That is, religion is their vision of what a perfect society would be. According to Durkheim, religion serves three important functions that benefit society as a whole: social cohesion, social control, and providing meaning and purpose. Religion improves social cohesion by bringing people together for shared religious participation, and by emphasizing the boundaries between acceptable and unacceptable behavior. By using ideas to promote conformity to societal norms, religion strengthens social control. Perhaps the most important function of religion is to answer questions of ultimate meaning concerning

birth, death, and the place of humans in the universe.

Another theoretical perspective that sociologists use to explain religion is symbolic-interaction analysis. This approach assumes that religion is a social construction that supports shared meanings and social definitions. Religion is created by society as a reflection of collective views of the way things are and the way they should be.

A third theoretical perspective is social-conflict analysis, which looks at religion as a bulwark of social inequality. According to this approach, religion supports the status quo by diverting attention away from patterns of inequality and domination. Karl Marx summarized this approach when he referred to religion as "the opium of the people." In addition, social-conflict theorists point out that most of the world's religions are patriarchal—dominated by men—thus perpetuating the inequality and domination of women.

Although religion often acts to support the status quo, it can also serve as an agent of social change. German sociologist Max Weber pointed out that the Calvinist belief in predestination was an important factor in the rise of industrialization in Western Europe in the centuries following the Middle Ages. A modern example of the power of religion to create social change is Liberation Theology, a Latin American religious movement that combines Catholicism with Marxist-based social activism.

Sociologists divide religious organizations into churches, sects, and cults. *Churches* are large reli-

71

gious organizations that are well integrated into the larger society. They are usually conservative in tone, and support the existing arrangements of society as a whole. The six major world religions—Christianity, Judaism, Islam, Confucianism, Buddhism, and Hinduism—include about four billion believers. In contrast, *sects* set themselves in opposition to society. Members hold strict religious convictions and consider themselves to be very different from persons who are not part of the sect. The Amish (Pennsylvania Dutch) are an example of a sect. *Cults* are small, often short-lived religious organizations that are typically organized around a charismatic leader. Their beliefs are often considered extreme by members of the larger society.

Religion is found in every society of the world, and in every historical time period. Sociologists point out that the type of religion that a society exhibits is related to the way in which the society produces food. Hunting/gathering societies often develop religions based on *animism*—the belief that forests, the sun, the wind, and other aspects of the natural environment are conscious life forms that influence humans. Pastoral and horticultural societies often base their religious beliefs on the idea of a single all-powerful god. The importance of religion to agrarian societies is illustrated by the huge cathedrals of medieval Europe. Even in industrial and postindustrial societies, religion continues to be important as a source of answers to questions of ultimate meaning—questions that science cannot address.

About 85 percent of adults in the United States identify with a particular religion, which is more than in most other industrial nations. In spite of this, only about 29 percent attend religious services on a weekly basis. Sociologists point out that religious affiliation is related to social class, ethnicity, and race. Members of certain religious groups tend to have high social standing while members of other groups tend to have a lower position on the social class ladder. Religion is related to ethnicity because members of religious groups often share a particular ethnic heritage. In the United States, race has been important for African-Americans who have used church participation to build social and political ties in local communities.

Secularization is the historical decline in importance of the supernatural and the sacred. It is often seen in advanced industrial or postindustrial societies where science is the dominant cultural mode of explanation. Even though modern societies are more secular than earlier societies, religion continues to be important in people's lives. *Fundamentalism*—a conservative religious movement that seeks to restore traditional beliefs and practices—continues to gain adherents. Some people search for spirituality on an individual basis outside of organized religious organizations. Others combine aspects of different religions, as illustrated in the video "In God We Trust" (Episode 17), where we see residents of New Orleans combining aspects of Catholicism and Voodoo. People also may participate in civil religion, which is the application of quasi-religious rituals and symbols, such as the American flag, to secular society. Immigrants will continue to bring their religious beliefs and practices from their home countries, which will intensify and diversify religion in the United States in the twenty-first century.

FOCUS YOUR ATTENTION

Assignments

Read the pages indicated for the text assigned by your instructor.

— *Sociology,* 10th Edition, by Macionis. Chapter 19, "Religion," pages 488–515.

— *Society: The Basics,* 8th Edition, by Macionis. Chapter 13, "Family and Religion," pages 363–379.

Watch Episode 17, "In God We Trust," after scanning the Video Focus Points.

Learning Objectives

After completing your study of this lesson, you should be familiar with the facts and concepts presented and should be able to:

1. Discuss the difference between the sacred and the profane.

2. Explain the views of the structural-functional, symbolic-interaction, and social-conflict theories on religion.

3. Describe the differences between churches, sects, and cults.

4. Explain the concepts of religiosity and secularization, and how they are reflected in the extent to which people participate in organized religious groups.

5. Explain how the relationship between Catholicism and Voodoo illustrates cultural influences on religion.

Key Terms and Concepts

The following terms are important to your understanding of the material presented in this lesson. Terms appearing only in the video are defined.

animism
charisma
church
civil religion
cult
denomination
faith
fundamentalism
liberation theology
profane
religion
religiosity
sacred
sect
secularization
state church
totem

Video Focus Points

The following points are designed to help you get the most out of the video for this lesson. Read them carefully before viewing the episode.

— Religion and culture are intertwined. Voodoo contains many elements of Catholicism adopted by African slaves who were prevented from practicing their own religion.

— Both Catholicism and Voodoo contain rituals and traditions.

— A primary function of religion is to provide meaning for human lives and to answer ultimate questions concerning death, suffering, and evil.

— Religion has been an important part of American life for centuries. Immigrants bring many diverse religions that become a part of the American religious landscape. Many Americans consider themselves spiritual but do not participate in organized religious groups.

— The United States Constitution requires the separation of church and state, but religion is a potent influence in American life.

Text Focus Points

These are the main points presented in the text assignment for this lesson. Read them carefully before reading the text.

— Religion is an important social institution, grounded in faith and involving sacred objects, events, and experiences.

— Religion provides answers to questions of ultimate meaning, and makes life less uncertain.

— Religion tends to support social inequality and unequal power relationships.

— Religious organizations can be divided into churches, sects, and cults.

— Most people in the United States view themselves as religious, but less than a third attend religious services regularly.

Critical Thinking Questions

These activities are designed to help you examine the material in this lesson in greater depth.

1. Discuss the question of faith versus science as competing systems of understanding.

2. Most people in the United States claim to believe in a supreme being, but less than a third participate in organized religion on a regular basis. Explain this apparent contradiction.

3. Discuss the issue of school prayer. Should prayer be allowed in schools even though the Constitution mandates the separation of church and state?

TEST YOUR LEARNING

After answering the following questions, check your responses against the answer key at the end of this book. Review any questions that you answered incorrectly.

Multiple Choice

1. Religion is based on _____, which is defined as "that which people set apart as extraordinary, inspiring awe and reverence."
   a. the magical
   b. the totemic
   c. the profane
   d. the sacred

2. Members of religious groups commonly participate in formal ceremonial behaviors known as
   a. sacrifices.
   b. elements.
   c. rituals.
   d. solidarities.

3. Religion is based on which of the following?
   a. Faith
   b. Reason
   c. Science
   d. Experience

4. Sociologists consider religion to be
   a. an organization.
   b. a bureaucracy.
   c. a social institution.
   d. a social role.

5. Which of the following points of view do sociologists adopt toward religion?
   a. Religion is wrong because it is not scientific.
   b. God does not exist, because the existence of God cannot be scientifically proven.
   c. Religion is the same as magic.
   d. Religion is a social institution that can be studied like other social institutions.

6. Which sociological thinker viewed society itself as godlike, because society survives the deaths of its members and shapes their lives?
   a. Emile Durkheim
   b. Karl Marx
   c. Herbert Spencer
   d. Max Weber

7. Which of the following is NOT one of the functions of religion as identified by Emile Durkheim?
   a. Social cohesion
   b. Social control
   c. Social change
   d. Providing meaning and purpose

8. According to the structural-functional approach, everyday objects that people transform into sacred symbols of their collective life are
   a. artifacts.
   b. totems.
   c. taboos.
   d. commodities.

9. According to the video "In God We Trust" (Episode 17), the Voodoo religion in New Orleans has strong connections to
   a. methodism.
   b. witchcraft.
   c. Catholicism.
   d. Judaism.

10. Which theoretical perspective assumes that religion, like all of society, is socially constructed?
    a. The structural-functional approach
    b. The symbolic-interaction approach
    c. The social-conflict approach
    d. The liberation theology approach

11. The civil rights movement, the student protest movement, the women's movement, and protests against the Vietnam War in the 1960s and 1970s resulted in
    a. a greater level of religious participation.
    b. a decline in respect for the authority structure of society.
    c. an increase in the number of persons receiving graduate degrees.
    d. a decline in the number of persons studying to become Catholic priests.

12. Which of the following is a criticism that applies to both the structural-functional approach and the symbolic-interaction approach?
    a. They don't place enough emphasis on power differences between groups.
    b. They place too much emphasis on power differences between groups.
    c. They do not explain the functions served by social institutions.
    d. They ignore the issue of socially-constructed meaning.

Short Answer

13. Explain the effect that increasing numbers of immigrants will likely have on religion in the United States.

14. Discuss Max Weber's view that Calvinist doctrine was an important influence on the rise of industrialism in Western Europe.

15. Discuss the differences between a church, a sect, and a cult.

Learning Curves

OVERVIEW

Education is a social institution through which society provides its children with factual information, job skills, and cultural norms and values. In high-income nations such as the United States, most formal education occurs as *schooling*, which is formal instruction under the direction of specially trained teachers. The availability of schooling is limited in low-income nations.

Since 1918, school attendance has been mandatory for American children 16 years of age and under. Most students attend public schools that are funded by tax dollars. Private schools are an alternative some parents choose for their children, and for which they must pay.

Structural-functional analysis suggests that schooling benefits all members of society. Important functions of education include socialization, cultural innovation, social integration, and social placement. Latent functions include providing child care for working parents, preventing students from competing with adults for scarce jobs, and bringing together people of marriageable age.

The social-conflict approach argues that schooling is closely related to social inequality, which means that only some groups benefit while others are poorly served. The amount of money spent per student is based on the socioeconomic status of the neighborhood, which varies widely throughout the United States. Private schools require parents to pay tuition, which limits the alternatives to the local neighborhood school for most families. Social-conflict analysis suggests that standardized tests are oriented toward the dominant culture, which puts minority students at a further disadvantage. Finally, the tracking system is biased because students from higher-income families are usually placed in higher tracks while students from disadvantaged backgrounds receive access to fewer school resources.

There are over 4,000 colleges and universities in the United States, ranging from elite private universities to local community colleges. Completion of a college degree offers people more career options and higher salaries throughout their lives. But college expenses are a significant burden for many families. School is not just for kids either. In 2000 more than 88 million adults enrolled in some type of schooling, either for career enhancement or personal enrichment.

The American school has experienced serious problems in recent decades. Most significant is the increase in incidents of violence. Other issues include drop-out rates, poor academic performance, student passivity, bureaucratic over regulation, teacher shortages and high turnover rates, and *grade inflation*.

For some parents, *home schooling* offers a solution to the problems they see in public schools. For others, providing more schools to choose from is the answer to make schools more competitive and better for kids. This option allows parents to play a primary role in the education of their children, as shown in the video "Learning Curves" (Episode 18).

FOCUS YOUR ATTENTION

Assignments

Read the pages indicated for the text assigned by your instructor.

— *Sociology*, 10th edition, by Macionis. Chapter 20, "Education," pages 516–539.

— *Society: The Basics*, 8th edition, by Macionis. Chapter 14, "Education and Medicine," pages 380–395 and 412–414.

Watch Episode 18, "Learning Curves," after scanning the Video Focus Points.

Learning Objectives

After completing your study of this lesson, you should be familiar with the facts and concepts presented and should be able to:

1. Explain the importance of education as a social institution.

2. Understand the functions of schooling according to the structural-functional perspective.

3. Understand how schooling creates and maintains social inequality.

4. Explain the benefits of completing a college or university degree.

5. Discuss some pressing problems in today's schools, such as violence, drop-out rates, grade inflation, and student passivity.

6. Understand the issues of school choice, home schooling, and teacher shortages within the American educational system.

Key Terms and Concepts

The following terms are important to your understanding of the material presented in this lesson.

busing
charter school
education
functional illiteracy
grade inflation
home schooling
magnet school
mainstreaming
parochial schools
school choice
schooling
schooling for profit
social capital
standardized tests
tracking

Video Focus Points

The following points are designed to help you get the most out of the video for this lesson. Read them carefully before viewing the episode.

— Parents often struggle to ensure that their children receive a good education in the best school possible.

— Most choose public school, but some opt for private school or home schooling.

— America's schools are more violent places than in earlier decades.

— Access to education in the United States is stratified by such factors as social class, race, and geographic location.

Text Focus Points

These are the main points presented in the text assignment for this lesson. Read them carefully before reading the text.

— Education is a social institution that teaches factual information, job skills, and cultural norms and values.

— Most formal education in high-income nations takes place as schooling; formal instruction under the direction of specially trained teachers.

— Structural-functional analysis suggests that schooling provides important benefits to all members of society.

— The social-conflict approach suggests that schooling helps to create and maintain social inequality.

— Schools have been beset by numerous problems in recent years, including elevated levels of violence, teacher shortages and high turnover rates, poor academic performance, student passivity and dropping out of school, and grade inflation.

— As a solution to some of the problems encountered in the American public school system, many parents are lobbying for more options in schooling their children, while others have opted to leave the educational system all together and home school their children.

Critical Thinking Questions

These activities are designed to help you examine the material in this lesson in greater depth.

1. Do you think that grade inflation is a serious problem in America's schools? Why or why not? If you do think it is a problem, what do you think can be done about it?

2. Why do many college students sit passively during class? How can faculty encourage students to participate in classroom discussion and debate?

3. To what extent do Americans enjoy equal access to schooling at the Kindergarten through 12th grade level and at the college level?

TEST YOUR LEARNING

After answering the following questions, check your responses against the answer key at the end of this book. Review any questions that you answered incorrectly.

Multiple Choice

1. The amount and type of schooling that a nation's citizens receive is closely related to its
   a. level of economic development.
   b. membership in the United Nations.
   c. primary type of family structure.
   d. state regulation of teacher certification.

2. The Greek root of the word *school* means
   a. work.
   b. sameness.
   c. leisure.
   d. training.

3. Illiteracy is most prevalent in
   a. Asia.
   b. Africa.
   c. Latin America.
   d. South America.

4. Why is the educational level of boys in India higher than the educational level of girls?
   a. Laws prohibit girls from attending school.
   b. Families encourage daughters to work instead of attend school.
   c. Educated women are seen as undesirable marriage partners.
   d. Indian boys are better students than Indian girls.

5. How do standardized tests transfer privilege into personal merit, according to the social-conflict approach?
   a. The tests measure skills needed for important jobs.
   b. The tests predict who will succeed in college.
   c. The tests raise academic standards for all students.
   d. The tests reflect the dominant culture.

6. According to the textbook, the American educational system has traditionally emphasized which of the following?
   a. Practical learning
   b. Basic research
   c. Political correctness
   d. Critical thinking

7. According to the structural-functional perspective, schools bring many diverse groups together into one society that shares norms and values. Which function of schooling does this illustrate?
   a. Socialization
   b. Cultural innovation
   c. Social integration
   d. Social placement

8. According to the video "Learning Curves" (Episode 18), the role that education plays in Americans' success today is
   a. less important than it once was.
   b. about as important as it once was.
   c. slightly more important that it once was.
   d. significantly more important than it once was.

9. Jonathan Kozol believes that _____ is one of the "savage inequalities" of the American school system because it discriminates against students from lower-class backgrounds.
   a. the school curriculum
   b. the tracking system
   c. the property tax
   d. the middle school

10. How much money, on average, does completing a four-year degree add to a person's lifetime earnings in the United States?
    a. $250,000–$350,000
    b. $450,000–$750,000
    c. $500, 000–$1,000,000
    d. $2,000,000–$8,000,000

11. What is the most significant change that has occurred in the school environment in recent years?
    a. More language policy infractions
    b. More dress policy infractions
    c. More violence in schools
    d. More racial segregation

12. The social-conflict approach has been criticized for ignoring
    a. how school provides upward mobility for all talented persons.
    b. the link between family income and educational attainment.
    c. the role of community colleges.
    d. private schools.

Short Answer

13. How are American schools different now than in previous decades?

14. How does schooling contribute to the smooth functioning of society as a whole, according to the structural-functional perspective?

15. How does schooling cause and perpetuate social inequality, according to the social-conflict perspective?

Taking the Pulse

OVERVIEW

Until very recently in human history, individuals provided their own health care for themselves and their families. Medicine emerged as a social institution as societies became more productive and work became more specialized. The scientific medicine practiced today in the United States emerged only in the last 150 years.

Medicine focuses on combating disease and improving health. *Health* has both physical and social components, since society defines what constitutes health and illness. The way that health is defined by a society is affected by a number of factors that may change over time. Cultural patterns and standards as well as the levels of technological development and social inequality present in a society are all such variable factors.

Health has improved over the course of human history but vast differences exist in the health and life expectancy of persons in low-income countries and those in high-income countries. The World Health Organization reports that one in six people around the world suffer from serious illness due to poverty. In the world's poorest nations, half the children die before reaching adulthood. In contrast, most people in rich industrialized nations have higher living standards and enjoy better health. But there are still many people in high-income nations who experience poor health, and they disproportionately tend to be children, women, members of minority groups, and persons in the lower social classes. *Infant mortality*—the death of children under one year of age—for example, is twice as high among the poor as it is among the wealthy in the United States.

Preventable causes of death and ill health in the United States include cigarette smoking, eating disorders, and sexually transmitted diseases. Tobacco smoking causes about 430,000 deaths each year. Victims of eating disorders are nearly all women, illustrating how the American cultural ideal of female beauty can create unrealistic standards. As illustrated in the video "Taking the Pulse" (Episode 19), HIV/AIDS is the most serious sexually transmitted disease. Since the outbreak of AIDS in 1981, over 468,000 U.S. residents have died of the disease. The problem is much worse worldwide, where AIDS constitutes a huge epidemic. Nearly 70 percent of the world's people who are living with HIV are in sub-Saharan Africa, where treatment is very expensive when it is available at all.

Every society must address ethical issues surrounding death. These include whether or not people have a right to die at a time of their choosing, and with the assistance of physicians through *euthanasia*. Currently only one U.S. state, Oregon, has legalized this practice and the issue is still being debated in Congress.

During the nineteenth century American physicians established strict legal and professional control over health care. The American Medical Association controls access to medical schools and professional licensing. Standards of medical care have improved greatly as technology has advanced and as scientific medicine has become the norm. Practitioners of *holistic medicine* offer an alternative, but they have often found themselves marginalized by the medical establishment.

Several models for paying health care costs exist among the nations of the world. They range from socialized, government-provided medical care like that found in Sweden, to the individual direct-fee system practiced in the United States. As the video points out, *health maintenance organizations* (HMOs) have been created to provide managed care, which combines prevention efforts with medical treatment and lowered costs. However, many people in the United States—especially those with lower incomes—have no health insurance, resulting in poorer health.

Three sociological theories offer ways of understanding health and medicine in our society. Structural-functional analysis suggests that illness is dysfunctional because it prevents people from performing necessary roles. According to this view, it is the job of physicians and patients to cooperate in regaining health in order to keep society operating smoothly. The symbolic-interaction approach views health and illness as social constructions that depend on cultural ideals. Adherents of the social-conflict approach focus on the level of inequality in society and how it results in differential access to health care for the rich and the poor.

FOCUS YOUR ATTENTION

Assignments

Read the pages indicated for the text assigned by your instructor.

— *Sociology*, 10th Edition, by Macionis. Chapter 21, "Health and Medicine," pages 540–567.

— *Society: The Basics*, 8th Edition, by Macionis. Chapter 14, "Education and Medicine," pages 395–415.

Watch Episode 19, "Taking the Pulse," after scanning the Video Focus Points.

Learning Objectives

After completing your study of this lesson, you should be familiar with the facts and concepts presented and should be able to:

1. Discuss four basic ways that society affects health.

2. Explain how health and illness differ in rich and poor nations.

3. Understand the threats tobacco, eating disorders, and sexually transmitted diseases pose to health.

4. Explain how the quality and level of health care vary within the United States and around the world.

5. Compare and contrast the explanations of health and health care offered by the structural-functional theory, symbolic-interaction theory, and social-conflict theory.

Key Terms

The following terms are important to your understanding of the material presented in this lesson. Terms appearing only in the video are defined.

Acquired Immune Deficiency Syndrome (AIDS)
euthanasia
health
health-maintenance organization (HMO)
holistic medicine
Human Immune Deficiency Virus (HIV)
medicine
scientific medicine
sick role
social epidemiology
socialized medicine

Video Focus Points

The following points are designed to help you get the most out of the video for this lesson. Read them carefully before viewing the episode.

— Acquired Immune Deficiency Syndrome (AIDS) is a serious chronic disease that illustrates the strengths and weaknesses of worldwide health care.

— Persons who are HIV-positive must contend with complex and expensive treatment programs, and they are often stigmatized by other members of society.

— Some countries provide free health care for all of their citizens while others, such as the United

States, require that people pay for their own care.

— Millions of people in the United States, including many members of minority groups and those with lower incomes, cannot afford basic health insurance.

Text Focus Points

These are the main points presented in the text assignment for this lesson. Read them carefully before reading the text.

— The way that society is organized affects definitions of health and illness, and the type of health care that people receive.

— Access to health care varies within nations, and from nation to nation.

— Health and illness are closely related to age, gender, race, and social class.

— About 40 million people around the world are infected with HIV, the virus that causes AIDS.

— Some nations offer their citizens free health care, while others require people to pay their own way.

Critical Thinking Questions

These activities are designed to help you examine the material in this lesson in greater depth.

1. Persons with AIDS, and those who are HIV-positive, have been subjected to a great deal of stigma and discrimination. Why do you think this is so?

2. Do you agree with symbolic-interaction theorists' assumption that health and illness are socially constructed? Why or why not?

3. Should the law allow parents to request DNA screening of their fetuses to predict the future health of their child? Why or why not?

TEST YOUR LEARNING

After answering the following questions, check your responses against the answer key at the end of this book. Review any questions that you answered incorrectly.

Multiple Choice

1. During the early twentieth century, people in tropical regions of Africa considered the skin disease yaws to be normal because it was so widespread. This is an example of which of the following ways that society affects health?
   a. Cultural patterns define health.
   b. Cultural standards of health change over time.
   c. A society's technology affects people's health.
   d. Social inequality affects people's health.

2. In 1854, researcher John Snow mapped the street addresses of London residents who had died of cholera and found that
   a. they lived in the same house.
   b. they lived in widely scattered locations throughout the city.
   c. they were treated with the same contaminated medicine.
   d. they drank water from the same well.

3. In 2000 the leading cause of death in the United States was heart disease. In 1900 the leading cause of death was
   a. stroke.
   b. accidents.
   c. influenza and pneumonia.
   d. disease in early infancy.

4. _____ is the study of how health and disease are distributed throughout a society's population.
   a. Social medicine
   b. Social demography
   c. Social epidemiology
   d. Social gerontology

5. According to the textbook, there is a gap of up to _____ years between the life expectancy of people in the richest communities of the U.S. and people in the poorest communities.
   a. 5
   b. 10
   c. 15
   d. 20

6. Which of the following social status categories is most strongly correlated with life expectancy?
   a. Educational level
   b. Race
   c. Gender
   d. Religion

7. Most American adults consider smoking to be
   a. socially acceptable.
   b. socially unacceptable.
   c. neither acceptable nor unacceptable.
   d. no research has been conducted on this issue.

8. More than one-third of the people in the nation of _____ now have AIDS.
   a. Russian Federation
   b. Botswana
   c. Libya
   d. Algiers

9. Which of the following involves dieting to the point of starvation?
   a. Bulimia
   b. Anorexia nervosa
   c. Binge eating disorder
   d. Low-carbohydrate dieting

10. What percentage of persons in the United States who suffer from eating disorders are women?
    a. 65 percent
    b. 75 percent
    c. 85 percent
    d. 95 percent

11. The great majority of people who are now living with the HIV virus reside in
    a. Africa.
    b. Eastern Europe.
    c. South America.
    d. Western Europe.

12. Which of the following is NOT a risk factor for HIV/AIDS?
    a. Anal sex
    b. Sharing needles
    c. Use of a drug
    d. Sharing dishes

Short Answer

13. What is managed care? What are some issues surrounding this method of providing health care?

14. Describe the extent of the worldwide HIV/AIDS epidemic. Which regions of the world have been most affected?

15. Compare and contrast scientific medicine and holistic medicine.

Rise and Fall

OVERVIEW

The study of human population—the size and composition of human societies and how people move from place to place—is termed *demography*. Basic demographic concepts include *fertility* (births), *mortality* (deaths), and *migration* (movement of people from one place to another).

For most of human history, population growth was very slow, and the total number of people relatively small. Beginning about 1750 the rate of population growth increased and the Earth's population reached one billion by 1800. During the late 19th century and throughout the 20th century the growth rate increased drastically. Overpopulation is now a serious global problem, with about 73 million people being added each year to the Earth's total population of 6.4 billion (2005).

Eighteenth century English economist Thomas Malthus believed that human populations grow geometrically while food supplies grow arithmetically. As a result, the Malthusian theory predicted, human populations will grow to levels that overtake the available food supply, resulting in starvation and war. *Demographic transition theory* is more optimistic, suggesting that societies can control overpopulation through technological development. Overpopulation is greatest in the poor nations of the Southern Hemisphere. Many such nations have made progress in lowering fertility rates, but these gains have been offset by decreases in mortality from improved health care, better sanitation, and new medicines such as antibiotics. Control of overpopulation requires even lower levels of fertility. The Northern Hemisphere, in contrast, has experienced a steady decline in growth rate in the centuries following the Industrial Revolution. The birth rate in the United

States is even below the replacement level, a situation demographers call *zero population growth*.

The Industrial Revolution caused a large migration of people from rural to urban areas. In the United States today, over 80 percent of U.S. American cities began to decline in population as city dwellers took advantage of automobiles and improved roads by moving to the *suburbs* in increasing numbers. This pattern is clearly illustrated by the recent history of Fresno, California, as shown in the video "Rise and Fall" (Episode 20). In many areas, cities and suburbs have grown together into large *metropolises* and these regions have merged with other metropolises to form huge *megalopolises* that stretch for hundreds of miles.

Tönnies, Durkheim, and Simmel suggested that the type of community solidarity found in the city is fundamentally different from that found in small rural areas. According to Tönnies the social organization of urban areas was based on association, what he called *Gesellschaft*. People only come together out of self-interest rather than kinship or tradition. Durkheim felt that urbanites did not lack social ties, but these ties were formed differently than those in rural areas. They were more based on specialization and interdependence. Simmel's researched focused on the need for city dwellers to become more blasé and detached from the world around them in order to cope with the crush of humanity that exists in a large city and allow individuals to save their compassion for those they care about. Scholars who adopt an urban ecology approach, like Robert Park and others from the Chicago School, see the city as a natural organism that develops according to an internal logic. This approach is criticized by the urban political-economy model, which focuses on the effects of power in defining city organization and city life.

The increase of global population in larger and larger settlements has taken a toll on our planet. Sociologists view Earth as a single global ecosystem that is influenced by all of the planet's residents regardless of the nation in which they live. As technology has become more sophisticated and widespread, an *environmental deficit* has developed, consisting of serious harm to the *natural environment* caused by people's focus on short-term material goals. The widespread human belief in growth and progress has led to depletion of natural resources and to mountains of solid waste. Water and air have become polluted and air quality is threatened by the cutting of tropical rain forests, which cleanse the environment of carbon dioxide.

In the years ahead, the people of the world must work together to create an ecologically sustainable culture; a way of life that meets the needs of the present generation without threatening the environmental legacy of future generations. Population growth must be brought under control, finite resources conserved, and solid waste levels reduced. As the video "Rise and Fall" (Episode 20) shows, issues of population, urbanization, and environment are truly global in scope, affecting people in developed nations and developing nations alike.

FOCUS YOUR ATTENTION

Assignments

Read the pages indicated for the text assigned by your instructor.

— *Sociology*, 10th Edition, by Macionis. Chapter 22, "Population, Urbanization, and Environment," pages 568–599.

— *Society: The Basics*, 8th Edition, by Macionis. Chapter 15, "Population, Urbanization, and Environment," pages 416–447.

Watch Episode 20, "Rise and Fall," after scanning the Video Focus Points.

Learning Objectives

After completing your study of this lesson, you should be familiar with the facts and concepts presented and should be able to:

1. Explain the major factors affecting human population size in the developed and developing nations of the world.

2. Compare and contrast the Malthusian and demographic transition perspectives on population growth.

3. Detail the rise of urbanization since the Industrial Revolution of the middle eighteenth century.

4. Discuss the views of Tönnies, Durkheim, Simmel, and Park on the nature of community and solidarity in cities.

5. Explain the interrelationships between culture, economic factors, and the natural environment.

Key Terms and Concepts

The following terms are important to your understanding of the material presented in this lesson.

age-sex pyramid
crude birth rate
crude death rate
demographic transition theory
demography
ecologically sustainable culture
ecology
ecosystem
environmental deficit
environmental racism
fertility
Gemeinschaft
Gesellschaft
global warming
infant mortality rate
life expectancy
megalopolis
metropolis
migration
mortality
natural environment
rain forests
sex ratio

suburbs
urban ecology
urbanization
zero population growth

Video Focus Points

The following points are designed to help you get the most out of the video for this lesson. Read them carefully before viewing the episode.

— The recent history of Fresno, California illustrates the changing nature of rural and urban life in the United States over the past half century.

— As cities grow larger, negative effects on the natural environment increase.

— People are becoming increasingly aware of the global nature of the natural environment.

— Population growth is a serious problem, especially in the poorest countries of the world.

Text Focus Points

These are the main points presented in the text assignment for this lesson. Read them carefully before reading the text.

— Demographers point out that human population size is influenced by fertility, mortality, and migration.

— Population growth has stabilized in the richer nations of the Northern Hemisphere, but it is a critical problem in the poorest nations of the Southern Hemisphere.

— Urbanization has occurred as human population size has increased and societies have become industrialized.

— Tönnies, Durkheim, Simmel, and Park point out that the nature of community and solidarity differs in large cities and small rural settings.

— The way in which societies organize their activities has profound global effects on the natural environment.

Critical Thinking Questions

These activities are designed to help you examine the material in this lesson in greater depth.

1. Which of the solutions to the problem of overpopulation proposed in this lesson do you believe is most workable? Why?

2. Must the growth of suburbs inevitably lead to the decline of cities? Why or why not?

3. What does it mean to say that the United States has become a disposable society?

TEST YOUR LEARNING

After answering the following questions, check your responses against the answer key at the end of this book. Review any questions that you answered incorrectly.

Multiple Choice

1. Sociologists who analyze the size and composition of a human population, and how people move from place to place, are known as
   a. gerontologists.
   b. demographers.
   c. migrationists.
   d. ecologists.

2. According to the textbook, a healthy woman is physically capable of bearing more than _____ children during her childbearing years.
   a. 7
   b. 12
   c. 20
   d. 30

3. Why is the crude birth rate described as "crude?"
   a. Because it is an inaccurate measure of fertility
   b. Because it is based on the entire population, not just women of childbearing age
   c. Because it is based only on the population of women of childbearing age, not on the entire population
   d. Because it does not take into account infant mortality

4. Life expectancy for North Americans is
   _____ than the typical life expectancy
   of people in low-income African countries.
   a. 2.5 years greater
   b. 25 years greater
   c. 25 years less
   d. 2.5 years less

5. An annual growth rate of two percent causes a
   doubling of the human population in
   a. 3.5 years.
   b. 35 years.
   c. 70 years.
   d. 105 years.

6. Why does the age-sex pyramid for lower-in-
   come nations tend to be wide at the bottom?
   a. High mortality
   b. Lack of health care
   c. High fertility
   d. Age discrimination

7. According to the video "Rise and Fall," Episode 20, which of the following was the primary cause of the decline of U.S. cities such as
   Fresno, California after the 1960s?
   a. Lax oversight by the federal government
   b. Changes in residential patterns resulting
      from increased automobile use
   c. The development of large department stores
      such as Wal-Mart
   d. The adoption of improved agricultural
      practices in surrounding areas

8. Thomas Malthus believed that human populations tend to grow geometrically rather than
   arithmetically. Which of the following is a geo-
   metric progression?
   a. 1, 2, 3, 4, 5
   b. 2, 4, 6, 8, 10
   c. 1, 3, 5, 7, 9
   d. 2, 4, 8, 16, 32

9. Demographic transition theory predicts that
   human population growth will be rapid when
   a society is in which of the following technological stages?
   a. Preindustrial
   b. Early industrial
   c. Mature industrial
   d. Postindustrial

10. Sociologists who study _____ analyze
    why cities are located where they are.
    a. political economy
    b. urban ecology
    c. zero population growth
    d. life expectancy

11. What has been the primary negative effect of
    the suburban real estate building boom in
    places like Fresno, California?
    a. Higher real estate prices in the central city
       area
    b. Fewer jobs for suburban workers
    c. Loss of agricultural land to housing devel-
       opments
    d. Higher taxes for all California residents

12. Sociologists refer to profound and long-term
    harm to the natural environment caused by
    humanity's focus on short-term material afflu-
    ence as
    a. an environmental deficit.
    b. global warming.
    c. an unbalanced ecosystem.
    d. the greenhouse effect.

Short Answer

13. How does the recent history of Fresno, Cali-
    fornia discussed in the video "Rise and Fall,"
    Episode 20, illustrate changes that have af-
    fected American cities during the past half
    century?

14. How do fertility and mortality influence hu-
    man population size?

15. What effect has technology had on Earth's
    natural environment?

LESSON 21

Mass Appeal

OVERVIEW

Organized activities designed to encourage or discourage social change are *social movements*. They involve planned efforts by social groups to achieve significant change in individuals or entire societies. The United States was formed by a social movement—the American Revolution. Examples of other social movements include the abortion rights and anti-abortion movements, the gay rights movement, the women's movement, the Civil Rights movement, and anti-war movements like the ANSWER Coalition depicted in the video, "Mass Appeal" (Episode 21) . Not all types of collective behavior constitute a social movement. Riots, for example, are not social movements because they are neither organized nor sustained.

Social movements vary according to who is being changed (individuals or all members of society) and how much change is being sought (limited change or total change). *Alternative social movements* attempt to achieve limited change among part of the population. An example is the Promise Keepers movement, made up of Christian men trying to lead more spiritual lives. *Reformative social movements* also seek limited change, but aim their efforts at the entire population of a nation or even the world. The environmental movement is one example of this type. Two other types of social movements seek widespread change in the structure of society as a whole. *Redemptive social movements* attempt to achieve profound change among selected individuals. The support group Alcoholics Anonymous is one such movement. Finally, *revo-lutionary social movements* seek total change in the structure of society. Movements of this type may include right-wing militia groups and left-wing utopian groups.

Social movements face a formidable task in developing organizational structures that allow them to sustain themselves and achieve their goals. As Francesca Polletta points out in the video, movements can be hierarchical and bureaucratic, or they can be egalitarian and democratic.

Sociologists have developed a number of theoretical perspectives in an attempt to explain the origin and development of social movements. *Deprivation theory* is based on the assumption that social movements will arise when people feel that they are not receiving their share of a valued resource such as money or political influence. This theory is based on the idea of *relative deprivation*, which is the notion that peoples' judgment of their level of deprivation is subjective and based on some type of comparison with other people or situations. *Mass-society theory* suggests that some social movement members are socially isolated, and that membership in the movement provides them with an identity and purpose. *Resource mobilization theory*, on the other hand, points to the key role of resources in determining the success of a social movement. The more members, money, and political influence that a social movement is able to attract, the more successful it is likely to be. *Culture theory* stresses the importance of symbols such as photographs, flags, and culturally-significant locations such as the site in New York City where the World Trade Center towers once stood ("ground zero"). Symbols can strengthen a movement by creating a strong emotional reaction and sense of community that can help sustain the movement. *New social movements theory* suggests that postindustrial society tends to spawn social movements that focus on quality-of-life issues on a global scale, such as world peace, the environment, or animal rights. The growth of these movements is encouraged by the power of the mass media and information technologies to unite people around the world to the same cause.

Sociologists point out that social movements usually proceed through a series of four stages during their life cycle. The first stage, *emergence,* arises when a group comes together in response to a shared reaction to some problem or condition. For example, the Civil Rights movement and the women's movement arose in response to a shared awareness of the powerlessness and subjugation of African Americans and women. The second stage of a social movement's life cycle is *coalescence.* Here the movement develops goals, recruits a solid membership base, and agrees on appropriate strategies and tactics. In the *bureaucratization* stage, the movement solidifies into a stable organization with a professional staff. The final stage, *decline,* occurs as the movement dies out from lack of resources, loss of interest, or because its goals have been achieved.

FOCUS YOUR ATTENTION

Assignments

Read the pages indicated for the text assigned by your instructor.

— *Sociology*, 10th Edition, by Macionis. Chapter 23, "Collective Behavior and Social Movements," pages 600–623.

— *Society: The Basics*, 8th Edition, by Macionis. Chapter 16, "Social Change: Modern and Postmodern Societies," pages 453–455.

Watch Episode 21, "Mass Appeal," after scanning the Video Focus Points.

Learning Objectives

After completing your study of this lesson, you should be familiar with the facts and concepts presented and should be able to:

1. Explain what social movements are and what they attempt to achieve.

2. Provide examples of historical and contemporary social movements.

3. Compare and contrast the different types of social movements: alternative, redemptive, reformative, and revolutionary.

4. Explain the basic assumptions of the various theories of social movements.

5. Explain what role the mass media play in shaping public opinion about social movements.

Key Terms and Concepts

The following terms are important to your understanding of the material presented in this lesson.

alternative social movement
bureaucratization
coalescence
culture theory
decline
emergence
mass society theory
new social movements theory
redemptive social movement
reformative social movement
relative deprivation theory
resource mobilization theory
revolutionary social movement
social movement

Terms undefined in the text:

collective identity – A sense of membership and loyalty in a group.

elite-led movements – Social movements led by professional staff, often having a paper membership rather than a participatory membership.

mass-based movements – Social movements with broad membership.

radical democracy – An organizational form in which all decisions are made by consensus.

tactics – Specific actions taken in order to achieve a certain goal.

targets – The particular institutions or situations at which social movements efforts are directed.

Video Focus Points

The following points are designed to help you get the most out of the video for this lesson. Read them carefully before viewing the episode.

— Social movements are organized and sustained efforts by large numbers of people to achieve broad social change.

— Participants in social movements develop a collective identity that enhances loyalty and solidarity with other participants.

— Social movements arise in response to a shared grievance and the hope that change can be achieved.

— Social movements vary in size, organizational form, type of leadership, level of activity, targets of action, and tactics.

Text Focus Points

These are the main points presented in the text assignment for this lesson. Read them carefully before reading the text.

— Social movements are organized activity that encourages or discourages social change. Examples include the American Revolution, the Civil Rights Movement, and the anti-abortion movement.

— There are four types of social movement: alternative, redemptive, reformative, and revolutionary. These types vary according to the nature of the change that is sought.

— Sociological explanations of social movements include deprivation theory, mass-society theory, resource mobilization theory, culture theory, and new social movements theory.

— Social movements usually proceed through the stages of emergence, coalescence, bureaucratization, and decline.

— The mass media are influential in shaping public opinion about social issues and social movements.

Critical Thinking Questions

These activities are designed to help you examine the material in this lesson in greater depth.

1. The Civil Rights Movement of the 1950s and 1960s resulted in significant advances for African Americans. Explain what type of social movement this was: alternative, redemptive, reformative, or revolutionary. Did the Civil Rights Movement exhibit characteristics of more than one of the above types?

2. Which type of social movement do you think is most threatening to the status quo? Give an example of a social movement of this type. Who might feel threatened by such a movement?

3. Deprivation theory suggests that the level of deprivation people feel is related to their expectations and to their comparisons with other people or other situations. Explain what relative deprivation means and give an example of a movement it fostered.

TEST YOUR LEARNING

After answering the following questions, check your responses against the answer key at the end of this book. Review any questions that you answered incorrectly.

Multiple Choice

1. A social movement is defined as organized activity that encourages or discourages
   a. social control.
   b. social change.
   c. social stratification.
   d. social conflict.

2. A social movement that seeks limited change to specific individuals is classified as
   a. an alternative social movement.
   b. a redemptive social movement.
   c. a reformative social movement.
   d. a revolutionary social movement.

3. A social movement that seeks radical change for everyone in society is classified as
   a. an alternative social movement.
   b. a redemptive social movement.
   c. a reformative social movement.
   d. a revolutionary social movement.

4. A social movement that seeks radical change for specific individuals rather than everyone in society is classified as
   a. an alternative social movement.
   b. a redemptive social movement.
   c. a reformative social movement.
   d. a revolutionary social movement.

5. A social movement that seeks limited change for everyone in society is classified as
   a. an alternative social movement.
   b. a redemptive social movement.
   c. a reformative social movement.
   d. a revolutionary social movement.

6. Alcoholics Anonymous is an example of
   a. an alternative social movement.
   b. a redemptive social movement.
   c. a reformative social movement.
   d. a revolutionary social movement.

7. The environmental movement seeks to mobilize widespread public support for environmental protection issues. The environmental movement is an example of
   a. an alternative social movement.
   b. a redemptive social movement.
   c. a reformative social movement.
   d. a revolutionary social movement.

8. The Civil Rights Movement, the anti-Vietnam War movement, and the women's movement are examples of
   a. revolutionary movements.
   b. resource mobilization movements.
   c. social movements.
   d. alternative social movements.

9. The successful effort by America's Founding Fathers to break away from Great Britain and form a new nation is an example of
   a. an alternative social movement.
   b. a redemptive social movement.
   c. a reformative social movement.
   d. a revolutionary social movement.

10. Promise Keepers is a group of Christian men who strive to be more spiritual and to be more supportive of their families. Promise Keepers is an example of
   a. an alternative social movement.
   b. a redemptive social movement.
   c. a reformative social movement.
   d. a revolutionary social movement.

11. Which of the following would NOT be an activity of a social movement?
   a. A Ku Klux Klan rally
   b. A boycott of businesses that do not hire senior citizens
   c. A women's march for equal rights
   d. A riot at a soccer game

12. Which of the following theories suggests that people's objective circumstances are less important in determining their levels of satisfaction than their subjective perceptions of their situation?
   a. Relative deprivation theory
   b. Mass-society theory
   c. Resource mobilization theory
   d. New social movements theory

Short Answer

13. Explain why the 1954 Supreme Court decision in *Brown v. Board of Education* was an important factor in the rise of the Civil Rights Movement.

14. Discuss some of the benefits of structuring a social movement with a participatory, democratic, consensus-based type of organization.

15. Why was the case of the Cracker Barrel firings of 1991 important for the issue of workers' rights?

Waves of Change

OVERVIEW

Social change is the transformation of culture and social institutions over time. As Claude S. Fischer points out in the video "Waves of Change" (Episode 22), this concept refers to changes in how people live, such as the size of their families, their lifestyles, and the kind of work they do. The process of social change exhibits four major characteristics. Social change is continual. It is sometimes intentional but often unplanned. It is frequently controversial because people and groups disagree over which changes are desirable. Some types of change, such as the invention of the computer, are more important than others, like clothing fads.

Social change may be caused by the *invention* of new objects, ideas, or social patterns, or it may occur through the *discovery* of existing elements of the world. The *diffusion* of products, people, and information from one society to another is another cause. Change can be set in motion by the *ideas* of charismatic leaders, like Martin Luther King, Jr., as well as *demographic shifts*, which often result in profound social change as people migrate from rural to urban areas or from one country to another.

Modernity refers to social patterns arising from the changes experienced as a result of the Industrial Revolution, which began in Western Europe during the mid-eighteenth century. Since that time modernity has produced a decline in small and traditional communities and an increase in large urban centers. Individuals have enjoyed greater personal choice and societies have become more tolerant of diversity as tradition has loosened its hold. Modernity means a focus on the future rather than the traditions of the past.

Four classical social thinkers have offered views of the modernization process. Tönnies suggested that modernization produces a loss of community as tradition is replaced by self-interest. Durkheim outlined the differences in group solidarity in traditional societies (mechanical solidarity) as compared to advanced societies (organic solidarity). Weber's approach focused on the importance of bureaucratic rationality in modern societies, while Marx emphasized the key role of social class in capitalist economies.

Structural-functional theory and social-conflict theory offer broad explanations of social change. Mass-society theory—a variation of the structural-functional approach—suggests that the increasing scale and complexity of modern life has produced many benefits, but that it has also resulted in a loss of individual ties to the community. Social-conflict analysis focuses on the social stratification in a class society that is brought on by modernity. It points to inequalities built into capitalist economic structures, and variations in power and resources among different groups.

Modernity has altered the lives of many individuals. Particularly important is the isolation and loss of identity in modern societies. According to David Riesman, people have moved from *tradition-directedness* to *other-directedness*. Paradoxically, modern societies give people more freedom from tradition, but they also cause individuals to be more powerless and socially isolated.

     People in Western societies often equate social change with progress. But modernity can produce great controversy and negative outcomes. The video "Waves of Change" (Episode 22) shows how the Winnemem Wintu tribe of the Pacific Northwest has been negatively impacted by U.S. Government water and land policies in the name of progress.

     Scholars use the term *postmodernity* to describe the society that has emerged from the Information Revolution. The Postmodernists who study this period view modern society as a failure in many ways because serious social problems such as poverty have not been solved. They point out that progress does not always accompany change, and they no longer believe that science will be able to solve important problems such as pollution. Postmodernists point to the increasing importance of ideas in postmodern society, as material objects become less important to those who have all the material objects they need.

     Social change is taking place all across the world. Modernization varies throughout the world, with some nations becoming prosperous and others exhibiting dire poverty. *Modernization theory* suggests that technological advances have produced great wealth for developed nations, and that developing nations should follow this model. *Dependency theory* is critical of this approach, pointing out the many difficulties faced by poor nations, including economic domination by the richer nations of the world.

FOCUS YOUR ATTENTION

Assignments

Read the pages indicated for the text assigned by your instructor.

— *Sociology*, 10th Edition, by Macionis. Chapter 24, "Social Change," pages 624–649.

— *Society: The Basics*, 8th Edition, by Macionis. Chapter 16, "Social Change," pages 448–474.

Watch Episode 22, "Waves of Change," after scanning the Video Focus Points.

Learning Objectives

After completing your study of this lesson, you should be familiar with the facts and concepts presented and should be able to:

1. Explain the nature of social change, its causes, and give historical and contemporary examples.

2. Show how the process of modernization (modernity) can result in positive and negative outcomes.

3. Discuss the perspectives on modernization and change offered by Tönnies, Durkheim, Weber, and Marx, and the perspective offered by the structural-functional and social-conflict analyses.

4. Discuss the controversial nature of social change as it affects individuals and groups within the United States and around the globe.

5. Discuss the rise and character of the postmodern era.

Key Terms and Concepts

The following terms are important to your understanding of the material presented in this lesson.

anomie
class society
division of labor
mass society
modernity
modernization
other-directedness
postmodernity
social change
social character
tradition-directedness

Video Focus Points

The following points are designed to help you get the most out of the video for this lesson. Read them carefully before viewing the episode.

— Social change can be beneficial to some groups while being harmful to others.

— Native American tribes such as the Winnemem Wintu struggle to maintain their identities in the face of continuing pressure from American society.

— Technological changes such as the invention of the automobile can have unintended and far-reaching consequences.

— Social change has affected all Americans in profound ways, and it will continue to do so in the future.

Text Focus Points

These are the main points presented in the text assignment for this lesson. Read them carefully before reading the text.

— Social change is the transformation of culture and social institutions over time.

— Causes of social change include invention, discovery, and diffusion.

— Industrialization produces modernization of society, with many associated processes of social change.

— In explaining modernization, Tönnies focused on community, Durkheim on the division of labor, Weber on the process of rationalization, and Marx on social inequality.

— People are less optimistic about the future in postmodern society than they were in the age of industrialization.

Critical Thinking

These activities are designed to help you examine the material in this lesson in greater depth.

1. How is social change related to the idea of progress? Give examples.

2. In what ways has the introduction of the automobile resulted in positive and negative change in U.S. society?

3. How has your own life been affected by changes brought about by the modernization process?

Test Your Learning

After answering the following questions, check your responses against the answer key at the end of this book. Review any questions that you answered incorrectly.

Multiple Choice

1. Which of the following is NOT an example of social change?
   a. Longer life expectancy
   b. Greater use of technology
   c. Increased levels of economic inequality
   d. All of the above are examples of social change

2. Most social change is
   a. intentional.
   b. beneficial.
   c. unplanned.
   d. unknown.

3. Which of the following is NOT one of the causes of cultural change that is discussed in the textbook?
   a. Invention
   b. Diffusion
   c. Discovery
   d. Community

4. The development of antibiotics to treat bacterial disease is an example of
   a. invention.
   b. discovery.
   c. diffusion.
   d. community.

5. The change in the average American household size from 4.8 people in 1900 to 2.6 people today is an example of
   a. demographic change.
   b. modernization.
   c. mechanical solidarity.
   d. the division of labor.

6. Which of the following is NOT one of the major characteristics of modernization identified by Peter Berger (1977)?
   a. Orientation toward the past
   b. Decline of traditional communities
   c. Expansion of personal choice
   d. Increased social diversity

7. Ferdinand Tönnies viewed modernization as a process of moving from
   a. *Gemeinschaft* to *Gesellschaft*.
   b. *Gesellschaft* to *Gemeinschaft*.
   c. society to community.
   d. agency to industry.

8. Emile Durkheim proposed that preindustrial societies are held together by similarities among people, which he referred to as
   a. organic solidarity.
   b. mechanical solidarity.
   c. class consciousness.
   d. anomie.

9. According to Claude S. Fischer in the video "Waves of Change," Episode 22, when sociologists talk about social change they are referring to
   a. medical advances.
   b. evolutionary changes in the human body.
   c. changes in the way people live.
   d. personality changes brought about over time.

10. Max Weber suggested that modern society is characterized by a high degree of
    a. tradition.
    b. rationality.
    c. anomie.
    d. inefficiency.

11. Most of the social change recently experienced by the Winnemem Wintu tribe highlighted in the video has been
    a. positive.
    b. negative.
    c. evolutionary.
    d. progressive.

12. Karl Marx believed that the inevitable fate of capitalist societies is
    a. slavery.
    b. revolution.
    c. feudalism.
    d. postmodernism.

Short Answer

13. What is social change? Give examples.

14. Explain what sociologists mean when they describe postindustrial societies as postmodern.

15. Choose an example of cultural change and explain how it has resulted from invention, discovery, or diffusion.

Answer Key

The title for the section in the text in which the answer can be found is indicated below. A "B" indicates the *Society: The Basics*," 8th edition text, and an "HB" indicates the *Sociology*, 10th edition text. If neither a "B" nor an "HB" is given, then the answer can be found in both books in the section title indicated.

Lesson 1: Connections

Multiple Choice

1. d The Sociological Perspective
2. b The Sociological Perspective
3. c Seeing Individuality in Social Context
4. a B: Seeing the Strange in the Familiar
   HB: Seeing Individuality in Social Context
5. b B: Seeing Individuality in Social Context
   HB: Sociology and Social Marginality
6. c Benefits of the Sociological Perspective
7. d The Origins of Sociology
8. b Science and Sociology
9. b Video
10. b Video
11. b B: Marginal Voices
    HB: Gender and Race: Marginal Voices
12. b The Social-Conflict Paradigm

Lesson 2: Truth Be Told

1. b B: Scientific Sociology
   HB: Science as One Form of Truth
2. d B: Scientific Sociology
   HB: Common Sense Versus Scientific Evidence
3. a Concepts, Variables, and Measurement
4. a Concepts, Variables, and Measurement
5. a Concepts, Variables, and Measurement
6. c B: Correlation and Cause
   HB: Concepts, Variables, and Measurement
7. c Video

8. c B: Correlation and Cause
   HB: Relationships among Variables
9. a B: Correlation and Cause
   HB: Relationships among Variables
10. c B: The Ideal of Objectivity
    HB: The Ideal of Objectivity
11. c B: Critical Sociology
    HB: A Third Framework: Critical Sociology
12. d Video

Lesson 3: Common Ground

1. c What is Culture?
2. b The Components of Culture
3. b Language
4. d Values and Beliefs
5. d Values and Beliefs
6. a "Ideal" and "Real" Culture
7. b Video
8. d B: Cultural Diversity
   HB: Cultural Diversity: Many Ways of Life in One World
9. a B: Cultural Diversity
   HB: Cultural Diversity: Many Ways of Life in One World
10. d High Culture and Popular Culture
11. b Video
12. d Ethnocentrism and Cultural Relativism

Lesson 4: Fitting In

1. d Social Experience: The Key to Our Humanity

2. a   Social Experience: The Key to Our Humanity
3. c   Social Isolation
4. b   Understanding Socialization
5. c   Understanding Socialization
6. d   Understanding Socialization
7. c   Understanding Socialization
8. b   Understanding Socialization
9. a   Video
10. c   Understanding Socialization
11. d   Understanding Socialization
12. a   Video

Lesson 5: Face to Face

1. c   Social Structure: A Guide to Everyday Living
2. b   Role
3. c   Status
4. c   Status
5. c   Role
6. a   Role
7. c   Video
8. c   The Social Construction of Reality
9. d   Dramaturgical Analysis: "The Presentation of Self"
10. a   B: Gender and Performance
       HB: Gender and Personal Performance Video
11. a   Emotions the Social Construction of Feeling
12. c   Interaction in Everyday Life: Three Applications

Lesson 6: All Together

1. c   Social Groups
2. a   Social Groups
3. a   Social Groups
4. a   Social Groups
5. c   Group Leadership
6. b   Group Conformity
7. b   Group Conformity
8. a   Group Size

9. d   Video
10. b   Social Diversity : Race, Class, and Gender
11. c   Video
12. a   B: Problems of Bureaucracy
       HB: Formal Organizations Oligarchy

Lesson 7: Against the Grain

1. d   The Social Foundations of Deviance
2. d   B: What is Deviance?
       HB: Social Control
3. b   The Social Foundations of Deviance
4. c   The Functions of Deviance: Structural-Functional Analysis
5. a   B: Durkheim's Basic Insight
       HB: Emile Durkheim: The Functions of Deviance
6. d   Merton's Strain Theory
7. b   Labeling Theory
8. c   The Medicalization of Deviance
9. d   Video
10. a   Sutherland's Differential Association Theory
11. d   Video
12. a   Video

Lesson 8: Matters of the Flesh

1. c   Understanding Sexuality
2. a   Sex: A Biological issue
3. a   Sex and the Body
4. d   Sex and the Body
5. c   The Incest Taboo
6. b   The Sexual Revolution
7. b   The Sexual Revolution
8. d   Video
9. b   The Sexual Revolution
10. c   The Sexual Revolution
11. b   The Sexual Counterrevolution
12. a   Video

Lesson 9: Ups and Downs

1. a   B: What is Social Stratification?

HB: What is Social Stratification? (Chapter 10)

2. b B: What is Social Stratification?
HB: What is Social Stratification? (Chapter 10)

3. d B: The Caste System
HB: The Caste System (Chapter 10)

4. d B: The Class System
HB: The Class System (Chapter 10)

5. b B: Critical Thinking, "Is Getting Rich the Survival of the Fittest"
HB: Critical Thinking, "Is Getting Rich the Survival of the Fittest" (Chapter 10)

6. b B: The Davis-Moore Thesis
HB: The Davis-Moore Thesis (Chapter 10)

7. b B: Stratification and Conflict
HB: Stratification and Conflict (Chapter 10)

8. b Video

9. d B: Social Classes in the United States
HB: Social Classes in the United States (Chapter 11)

10. d B: The Difference Class Makes
HB: The Difference Class Makes (Chapter 11)

11. b B: Social Mobility
HB: Social Mobility (Chapter 11)

12. d Video

Lesson 10: Worlds Apart

1. d Global Stratification: An Overview
2. b A Word About Terminology
3. a A Word About Terminology
4. d Global Stratification: An Overview
5. a The Severity of Poverty
6. b The Severity of Poverty
7. c The Severity of Poverty
8. d Video
9. c The Severity of Poverty
10. a Slavery
11. c Video
12. b Video

Lesson 11: Venus and Mars

1. c Gender and Inequality
2. d Male-Female Differences
3. d Gender Stratification, Introduction
4. c Male-Female Differences
5. a Patriarchy and Sexism
6. b Patriarchy and Sexism
7. b Video
8. b Gender and Socialization
9. c Working Women and Men
10. c Working Women and Men
11. a Video
12. c Gender and the Military

Lesson 12: Colors

1. a Race
2. c Racial Types
3. c Discrimination
4. b White Ethnic Americans
5. c Institutional Prejudice and Discrimination.
6. b Minorities
7. a Assimilation
8. d Video
9. a Video
10. d Theories of Prejudice
11. a Theories of Prejudice
12. d Native Americans

Lesson 13: Golden Years

Unless otherwise stated the answers in the hardback text come from Chapter 15, "Aging and the Elderly."

1. a B: Chapter 3, "Socialization", Erik H. Erikson: Eight Stages of Development
HB: Chapter 5,"Socialization: From Infancy to Adulthood" Erik H. Erikson: Eight Stages of Development

2. b B: Chapter 3, "Socialization: from Infancy to Old Age," Old Age
HB:Growing Old: Biology and Culture

3. a   B: Chapter 3, "Socialization: from Infancy to Old Age," Old Age
        HB: Age Stratification: A Global Survey

4. c   B: Chapter 3, "Socialization: from Infancy to Old Age," Old Age, Death and Dying
        HB: Bereavement

5. a   B: Chapter 8, "Social Stratification," Who Are the Poor?
        HB: Aging and Poverty

6. b   B: Chapter 15, "Population, Urbanization, and the Environment," Mortality
        HB: An Aging Society: Cultural Change

7. d   Video

8. b   B: Chapter 13, "Family and Religion", The Family in Later Life
        HB: The "Young Old" and the "Old Old"

9. a   B: Chapter 8, "Social Stratification", Who Are the Poor?
        HB: Diversity Snapshot, U.S. Poverty Rates by Age, 2001

10. d   B: Chapter 14, Education and Medicine, Ethical Issues Surrounding Death
        HB: Ethical Issues: Confronting Death

11. c   Video

12. a   B: Chapter 14, "Education and Medicine," Health in the United States
        HB: Historical Patterns of Death

Lesson 14: Working World

1. a   The Agricultural Revolution

2. b   Sectors of the Economy

3. a   Relative Advantages of Capitalism and Socialism

4. d   The Global Economy

5. a   B: The Changing Workplace
        HB: The Decline of Agricultural Work

6. d   Professions

7. b   Video

8. a   B: Workplace Diversity: Race and Gender
        HB: Box, p. 422: Diversity: Race, Class, and Gender

9. c   Labor Unions

10. d   The Industrial Revolution

11. c   Video

12. b   Welfare Capitalism and State Capitalism

Lesson 15: Balance of Power

1. a   B: Global Political Systems
        HB: Politics in Global Perspective

2. b   B: Global Political Systems
        HB: Politics in Global Perspective

3. b   Politics in the United States

4. d   B: Global Political Systems
        HB: Politics in Global Perspective

5. d   Politics in the United States

6. c   B: Theoretical Analysis of Politics
        HB: Theoretical Analysis of Power in Society

7. c   Video

8. d   Politics in the United States

9. c   Politics in the United States

10. b   Special-Interest Groups

11. d   Video

12. b   Politics in the United States

Lesson 16: Family Matters

1. c   Marriage Patterns

2. b   The Family: Global Variations

3. a   The Family: Basic Concepts

4. d   The Family: Basic Concepts

5. b   The Family: Global Variations

6. b   Theoretical Analysis of the Family

7. a   Video

8. b   Alternative Family Forms

9. d   Alternative Family Forms

10. d   Transitions and Problems in Family Life

11. c   Video

12. d   Transitions and Problems in Family Life

Lesson 17: In God We Trust

1. d   Religion: Basic Concepts

2. c   B: Religion: Basic Concepts
        HB: Religion and Sociology

3. a   Religion: Basic Concepts

4. c   Religion: Basic Concepts

5. d   B: Religion: Basic Concepts
        HB: Religion and Sociology

6. a Functions of Religion: Structural-Functional Analysis
7. c Functions of Religion: Structural-Functional Analysis
8. b Functions of Religion: Structural-Functional Analysis
9. c Video
10. b Constructing the Sacred: Symbolic-Interaction Analysis
11. b Video
12. a Theoretical Analysis of Religion

Lesson 18: Learning Curves

1. a Education: A Global Survey
2. c Education: A Global Survey
3. b Window on the World, Global Map, Illiteracy in Global Perspective
4. b Schooling in India
5. d Schooling and Social Inequality, Video
6. a Schooling in the United States
7. c The Functions of Schooling
8. d Video
9. b Schooling and Social Inequality
10. c Access to Higher Education
11. c Video
12. a Privilege and Personal Merit

Lesson 19: Taking the Pulse

1. a Health and Society
2. d Health in High-Income Countries
3. c The Leading Causes of Death in the United States, 1900 and 2002
4. c B: Life Expectancy Across the United States
     HB: Health Across the United States
5. d B: National Map 14-2, p. 384
     HB: Health in the United States
6. c Health in the United States
7. b Cigarette Smoking
8. b) Video
9. b Eating Disorders
10. d Eating Disorders
11. a Video
12. d Sexually Transmitted Diseases

Lesson 20: Rise and Fall

1. b Demography: The Study of Population
2. c Fertility
3. b Fertility
4. b Mortality
5. b Population Growth
6. c Population Composition
7. b Video
8. d History and Theory of Populations Growth
9. b Demographic Transition Theory
10. b Urbanism as a Way of Life
11. c Video
12. a Environment and Society

Lesson 21: Mass Appeal

1. b B: Social Movements and Change
     HB: Social Movements
2. a Types of Social Movements
3. d Types of Social Movements
4. b Types of Social Movements
5. c Types of Social Movements
6. b Types of Social Movements
7. c Types of Social Movements
8. c Video
9. d Types of Social Movement
10. a Types of Social Movements
11. d Video
12. a Explaining Social Movements

Lesson 22: Waves of Change

1. d What is Social Change?
2. c What is Social Change?
3. d Causes of Social Change
4. b Causes of Social Change
5. a Causes of Social Change
6. a Modernity
7. a Ferdinand Tönnies: Loss of Community
8. b Emile Durkheim: The Division of Labor
9. c Video
10. b Max Weber: Rationalization
11. b Video
12. b Karl Marx: Capitalism